KENPO

21

PRIORITY PRINCIPLES

By Roy Travert

DISCLAIMER

Although the author and publisher have made every effort to ensure that the information in this book was correct at press time, the author and publisher do not assume and hereby disclaim any liability to any party for any loss, damage, or disruption caused by errors or omissions, whether such errors or omissions result from negligence, accident, or any other cause. The information in this book is meant to supplement, not replace, proper tuition in Kenpo Karate training.

Like any sport involving speed, equipment, balance, and environmental factors, practicing Kenpo Karate poses some inherent risk. The author and publisher advise readers to take full responsibility for their safety and know their limits. Before practicing the skills described in this book, be sure that your equipment is well maintained, and do not take risks beyond your level of experience, aptitude, training, and comfort level. If in any doubt, consult with your doctor before commencing any form of exercise.

This book is not intended as a substitute for the medical advice of physicians. The reader should regularly consult a physician in matters relating to his/her health and particularly with respect to any symptoms that may require diagnosis or medical attention before they commence training.

No part of this book may be stored in a retrieval system, copied, or otherwise used without the prior consent of the author.

TABLE OF CONTENTS

DEDICATION

This book is dedicated to all security personnel who every day put their lives on the front line of violence, to protect and promote the safety of others.

KNOWLEDGE
Facts Information and Skills

"If we think of a key the first thing that comes to mind is it fitting a lock. Once the key is inserted and turned, the lock opens"

"If however, we used the wrong key, the lock would not open, the way to open all locks would be to use a Master Key"

ABOUT THE AUTHOR

Roy Travert started training in Ed Parker's Kenpo at the age of fifteen whilst he was still at school, he was educated at St Helier Boys School in Jersey, one of the Channel Islands located in the English channel nine miles from the French coast of Normandy. He has spent over thirty years studying and acquiring knowledge of the Kenpo system and its techniques. Throughout this learning process, he has trained with renowned Kenpo black belts Tony Martin, Jeff Speakman, John Sepulveda, Graham Lelliott, and Roy MacDonald, as well as various instructors that do not train in Kenpo but have contributed to his overall martial art development. By the age of twenty-three, he had attained the rank of 1st degree black belt under the tutelage of his instructor's Graham Lelliott and Roy MacDonald, gaining his black belt in the spring of 1989, the test was conducted in Plymouth England, and overseen by the Senior Grand Master of American Kenpo Edmund K Parker.

Working for the past 12 years in the nighttime security industry, he has witnessed hundreds of major as well as minor incidents. This has confirmed for him that putting into practice what you have learned in the Dojo is not the same as working in this type of hostile environment, where people have consumed vast quantities of alcohol and drugs. This has given him a practical realistic approach to his training in Kenpo, and how it should be applied on the street.

PREFACE

Kenpo School Badge - Copyright R. Travert

This book is about the application of Kenpo from my own personal perspective, and how after thirty years of training and working in the security industry, I have seen some horrendous violent crimes inflicted on innocent people and the damage that has been done to them. Life is full of violence, it is a fact of life. It is how you learn to deal with it that is important. Developing the correct mental, as well as physical fighting skills that contain valid proven principles of motion, based on scientific and practical experience, is essential to protect yourself in today's increasingly hostile society.

The following chapters will explain the twenty-one key principles that will enhance, aid, and improve the physical and mental skills taught in American Kenpo Karate. They are *priority principles* found in all martial art systems and can be used by anyone regardless of what they are learning. Having an in-depth knowledge of these principles entails having an understanding of physics and

1

how this knowledge will transfer into understanding the sophistication found in basic self-defense techniques. Ingraining them into your subconscious mind will increase the speed at which you retain information, and how it is understood and processed by the person learning it. The end goal of any practitioner is to develop this skill set to attain a flexible powerful and functional mindset. This is then complemented by the use of physical self-defense techniques.

Like most martial arts, Kenpo has a proven base of scientific principles and concepts. From a structured and well-defined technique base to a clearly written syllabus. Kenpo is a modern form of self-defense based on traditional values of honor, integrity, and respect. It draws from a martial arts legacy that is traditional in nature but modern in application. Modern day warfare is technologically advanced and conducted in many cases from afar, drone aircraft pinpoint targets from many miles away, striking with deadly accuracy and force. The target in many cases never knew they were about to be hit or die. Technology has moved the boundaries of warfare from fighting each other with rocks, spears, and swords, to a highly sophisticated accurate and deadly form of combat. New modern day technologies coexist with old forms of close protection that are just as effective and deadly today, as they were 100 years ago.

Although certain types of combat situations are the same in context, they may vary greatly in the way they are dealt with physically. If you are in a war zone, you may have no choice but to use deadly force to defend and protect yourself. Your response to a domestic situation using the same level of force could end up with you in a court case, and a life in prison at the end of it.

Techniques taught within self-defense schools have the capability to take life, in a domestic situation lethal force should be used as a last resort in any circumstance. For a lot of martial artists the idea that they might have to fight someone to the death to protect themselves or their family, does not enter their minds. Many people practice martial arts for fitness training and as a recreational past time; it is not life or death to them. They forget that the **Martial Arts** by definition means military or relates in some way to the armed forces. It is a name given to persons befitting that of a warrior.

The definition of **Art** is combined with **Martial** as it refers to the studies that people go through that provides the knowledge and intellectual skills for them to train and fight with. It is the thought process or the thinking side of training. The two elements co-exist side by side to complement each other through the training of both your mind and body. The importance of learning how to learn, cannot be overemphasized.

Throughout history, war and conflict have always forged new nations, China, America, Russia, France, Spain, and England have all felt the brutal effect this has had on its people and the country they live in. As I write this book, war is raging in the Middle East sending millions of people across Europe as refugees, fleeing hostile and deadly forces that would otherwise kill them. The need for self-defense training could not be greater than at this time in history. From one nation instigating the horrors of war on another, and the defense of nation-states, history provides us with lessons of defense and protection. From the ancient Knights of old England to the Samurai of Japan, great martial arts masters grew out of conflicts such as these. Having proven their fighting ability on the battlefield, they were revered throughout society for their physical ability and prowess.

In today's social environment, teaching self-defense skills to people is not the same as competing in a tournament with referees who are ready to stop the fight if one person is knocked out, or taken to the ground and ends up in a vulnerable prone position. If the same thing was to happen on the street, your attacker may not stop, with the very real possibility of causing you permanent life-changing injuries or take your life if they win. Learning effective practical self-defense skills is a way to protect you, your family, and loved ones. In most cases, this is based on a common sense approach to life, and all that may be needed is that you leave an area of provocation before any physical intervention is required. These simple life skills are taught to us as children as we grow up and passed down from one generation to the next for our own safety and protection.

"The secret to Kenpo is to have knowledge of motion and its components, then tailor it to the individual learning it"

SENIOR GRAND MASTER
ED PARKER

Ed Parker and Roy Travert Jersey 1989

No Kenpo book would be complete without reference to the creator of American Kenpo, Senior Grand Master Ed Parker. I was quite fortunate to not only have Mr. Parker sit on my grading panel and promote me to my 3rd brown belt, but I was also promoted to my 1st Degree black belt by him in Plymouth England. I remember being asked on his last visit to Jersey before his untimely passing, what subject we would like to cover whilst he was here. This was to be a black belt seminar so I immediately replied I would like him to cover some of the forms, namely Short Form 3 and Long Form 3. He spent the following sessions covering in the finest detail the content and application of the forms and why they were created. These were some of the last seminars that Mr. Parker taught and was fortunately preserved for history as they were video recorded by Neil Chadwick one of Graham Lelliott's black belts. Mr. Parker would spend time explaining not only the content and structure of the techniques the forms contained, but also the principles behind them, and why they would work in generating power in actual combat.

The late Mrs. Parker with Roy Travert at Fort Regent Jersey

He would always teach specific subjects with great precision and explain what each part of a technique should achieve and why you were practicing it. Always explaining the body mechanics used, and how power was generated through correct anatomical body alignment and the principals used to achieve it. He had an unparalleled ability to convey verbally exactly what we were expected to achieve physically. That made his style of teaching unique. He would always reiterate that when working a technique, you are analyzing a set or ideal phase self-defense situation and that it should be viewed not only from your point of view but from your opponents and that of a bystander as well. Above all, he would teach the correct application of proven principles of motion that would enhance your training and make you a better fighter. Although Mr. Parker wrote extensively about how to apply the many principles that the art contains, and authored countless books on the subject, the most notable are his **Infinite Insights into Kenpo** series, American Kenpo will always remain in a constant state of change and evolution, and always will be. However, as times change and certain techniques become practiced more than others and are tested in a real-world environment proving their worth to the system, others will become obsolete and removed from the syllabus.

Concepts and principles, are technical tools to help refine your motion

However, the underlining core principles that link motion and its subcomponents will always remain constant. Techniques will change due to the person practicing them, and the instructor that is teaching them, with some that are more suited to a certain body type than others, this is something that Mr. Parker recognized and allowed for in the Kenpo system he created. People are different, some will have certain abilities that are greater or less than others. This he knew would always lead people down the path of tailoring the system to the individual learning it, where they would ultimately create their own style.

Although Mr. Parker is no longer here to teach and instruct students of Kenpo, he left a lifelong legacy of instruction manuals and literature that clearly defines how to apply Kenpo in a real-world environment and how the principles his system contains should be applied in a logical and systematic manner to enhance your movement and increase your power. This will inevitably lead practitioners of the art down the path of the **FORMULATION PHASE** of a self-defense technique and the application of the **REARRANGEMENT CONCEPT**.

A concept is an idea.

A theory is an idea that is still speculative.

A principle is a theory that has been proven

I teach Kenpo, not for the sake of teaching the techniques, but for the principles involved in them.

Even then, these principles must be altered to fit the individual learning them.

Ed Parker

KENPO - FIST LAW

    The title given to our system of martial art translates into English as **"Law of the Fist"** or **"Fist Law."** Ken meaning fist and Po meaning Law. The title of the system is very clear, it means it is a fighting art, one that is based on the physical application of fighting techniques. When Mr. Parker commenced his training in Kenpo, he was learning a more traditional system which did not contain the techniques or forms that American Kenpo has in it today. As with everything in life, change is inevitable. He could see the need to restructure and modernize the Kenpo system he was learning, as the years progressed, he would bring in new forms and self-defense techniques. Building a new system of Kenpo that was more in sync with the American culture and mindset. He Americanized the traditional system of Kenpo he was learning, into a modern self-defense system with relevant modern training methods and self-defense techniques. Bringing together the traditional elements of the "old ways" and combining them together with "new elements" of training. People train in the martial arts for many different reasons, I started to train in Kenpo for one reason and one reason only, to protect myself on the street, and get fit. Everything else was secondary to learning how to kick and punch hard, without being hit myself. I must have spent thousands of hours over the past thirty odd years, training and developing my skill set. I have seen and trained with some great fighters from Kenpo, Freestyle Karate, and traditional Karate, and many others who went on a different path to learn ground-fighting skills. Regardless of the system they were learning they all had one thing in common, they could all fight.

A freestyle seminar in Guernsey that I taught with the FSKA School

By that, I mean they didn't know the same systems or the same techniques, but they knew body mechanics and where they should be to get in the best possible strategic position in a fight. They knew how to align their hips correctly to get the most power out of a punch or kick, and how to take you to the ground if they needed to.

The whole point of training in any martial art system is to get physically and mentally fit and strong from the training, the bottom line is if you ever need to fight, you have to have a certain amount of physical fitness to be able to do so. Failing to take care of this aspect of your training will most definitely have an adverse effect on your ability to defend yourself effectively on the street. Although it would be nice to imagine that everything we did in Kenpo resulted in the physical if not the mental destruction of our opponent, unfortunately, the reality of life and the physical limitations of our own bodies sometimes limits our ability to achieve this action. We can, however, be the best physically and mentally that we can be. When I was young and a newly promoted black belt, I trained with some of the world's top Kenpo instructors. The training in the eighties and nineties was extremely physical and very demanding on the body. The vast majority of the training sessions were 2 to 3 hours long and within each training session, we would cover a vast amount of material. Not only did we learn all our syllabus material, which included self-defense techniques, forms, and sparring, but we also spent a considerable amount of time on fitness training. I would train nearly every night, and by the end of the week, I was exhausted.

Pad training at a seminar with Gary "Smiler" Turner

It was tough. The only reason I would take any time off from training would be if I had picked up a serious injury or I was sick for some other reason, which wasn't often. I was young, keen, and hungry to learn anything and everything that was Kenpo and the martial arts. This is probably true of anybody that saw the Karate instructors at that time, who I have to say, were outstanding in their ability and knowledge. Not only did I train in Kenpo, but when the opportunity presented itself, I would also train with one of my other Kenpo instructors Nick Norie, who trained in Shukokai Karate as well. The head instructor of the school was Derek Veitch, who teaches under the name of Jersey Shito-Ryu Shukokai Karate Club. Mr. Veitch would have some of England's top instructors visit Jersey, and I would take the opportunity to take part in as many seminars as possible when they were on the island. Although they were training in a more traditional Karate system, the students and instructors could fight! Believe me, when I say that you did not want to be hit by them, they had solid punches, solid kicks, and boy they were fast! I found that by exposing myself to other streams of information it made me examine what I was really expecting to learn from my instructors and my training in Kenpo.

Roy Travert, Gary "Smiler" Turner (M.M.A), and Andrew Toporis

Training with other instructors from different styles was extremely objective for me. It led me to a very interesting junction in my own personal training in Kenpo. I was friends with many black belts from different systems and had many in-depth conversations with them about the systems they were learning, and the difference between them and Kenpo. After I tested for my black belt, I started to cross train in other martial arts schools. The main reason I did this was to increase my knowledge of other systems and how they were structured compared to Kenpo. I didn't really have any spare time to devote to another system of training full time, as each martial art has its own techniques, its own forms, if it has any at all, and its own way of presenting each subject. I was learning 24 self-defense techniques per belt level in Kenpo, this meant that you had to spend a considerable amount of time learning each technique to be competent in executing it. There simply wasn't enough time in the day to do everything, and the thought of learning another syllabus really did not appeal to me that much. Kenpo pretty much had everything I needed for my own self-protection, however, training in other systems certainly increased my understanding of the traditions and formalities that they contained and the solid foundation of basics that they are based on.

John Sepulveda (left) teaching a class in Jersey

What I gained from training in other schools, was the re-examining of my basics. Did they work? Were they good enough compared to another martial art system and instructors? Did they function properly and were they really going to be effective enough in a real fight? Or, was it all Hollywood flash with no substance?

It became very clear to me that what I was learning was practical and effective, and if I needed to add anything into my own personal vocabulary of motion, I had training partners with whom I trained with, that could fill any gaps that I might have had. If you have spent time training with more than one instructor, you will find they all have their own story to tell of how they chose the particular system they were learning, and how they themselves changed and developed over the years. This is the same for anyone that trains in the arts, and it will be the same for you if you are reading this book. However, one thing that remained constant throughout this learning process was basics and even more basics with lots of drills that defined each movement within them.

For years, I ran a Sunday morning sparring class at Fort Regent where instructors from many different systems would come and train, it was a platform to share knowledge and see if what we had learned, actually worked. The class format was very simple, warm up, drills, and fight. As far as I'm concerned, you must be able to stand in front of someone and spar with them. This is the only way you are going to know if all the basics, drills, and techniques you have learned actually work. You can use it as a barometer for your overall training and whether your skill set is actually increasing and getting better or not.

Groundwork with Matt Leech

Modern-day Kenpo has developed a core set of self-defense techniques that cover relevant practical applications based on scenarios found on the street. These techniques are primarily designed for street self-defense and contain the 21 key principles required to apply **BASICS IN MOTION**. Regardless of the system you are learning or the instructor teaching it, the following principles are key to developing power along with a solid foundation to train and fight from. They are applied to everything we do in Kenpo. Every self-defense technique contains these principles of motion and movement, whether you are practicing a form, sparring, or practicing self-defense technique, you will find that the execution of one principle will, in fact, trigger the remaining principles to be applied to whatever technique you are using. They will effectively enhance your strikes and blocks whilst you are in motion. When training try to develop basic principles that will benefit you the most in the shortest possible time. Principles that teach you to generate power should be at the top of your list. Other principles can be then added along with other concepts to enhance your overall training program.

POWER PRINCIPLES

Whether we are aware of it or not, whenever we use a block or strike, one of these three principles will come into play. At least one of them will be the overriding principle that will trigger other *priority principles* to be applied to any given technique.

MARRIAGE OF GRAVITY - Dropping your weight vertically using height.

TORQUE - Rotational energy using width.

BACKUP MASS - The use of body weight directly behind the action using depth.

If you wish to develop real power in your strikes and blocks, it is essential that you synchronize the rotation of your body whilst moving and dropping your body weight at the same time. This will engage all of your height, width, and depth zones which will ultimately increase power.

PRIORITY PRINCIPLES

The study of martial arts training is nothing new, regardless of the martial art you study, the principles of motion remain the same, you simply cannot change the laws of physics. Depending on the system you practice, or who the instructor is, they may teach a slightly different way to execute a technique or to do the same thing, but, so long as it contains power generating principles that use logic and common sense, then you are being taught Kenpo. You cannot change the basic principles of motion that are universally applied regardless of the system being studied or who is teaching it.

Making sure you rotate your hips to generate power, whilst keeping your guard up, is a **BASIC FUNDAMENTAL** that can be applied to all systems. A punch in Kenpo if delivered correctly, will generate as much damage to an opponent as a punch thrown by a Thai Boxer or an M.M.A fighter. Basic principles of motion remain the same for all forms of combat, they do however need to be applied consistently to ensure the effectiveness of your blocks and strikes when fighting. Many styles will teach low kicks, whilst other systems will concentrate on high kicks, punches, and sparring. However, they are all bound by the same scientific principles that include **GRAVITATIONAL MARRIAGE, TORQUE, BACKUP MASS,** and **SPEED.** Without the defined application of proven principles, you are just flailing your arms and legs around in an uncontrolled fashion.

Principles give meaning and definition to what you are doing, and how your blocks and strikes should be applied. The following principles form the base of all your movement, the more principles you can apply whilst fighting, the more power will be generated. Although the object is to apply all of these principles at the same time, the reality is that you may only be able to apply some but not all of them. You will, however, find that there are certain principles that are always used, regardless of the technique being applied or the position your opponent is in. These can be considered as *priority principles* that will always rise to the top of your list when being used. Principles that automatically generate power such as *Gravitational Marriage*, *Backup Mass*, and *Torque* when used with correct breathing techniques will solidify your posture and stance resulting in a more powerful practitioner.

21 PRIORITY PRINCIPLES

1. ERECT POSTURE
2. BALANCE
3. RELAX
4. SPEED
5. ACCURACY
6. ANGLES
7. BODY ALIGNMENT
8. BACK UP MASS
9. ECONOMY OF MOTION
10. TIMING
11. TELEGRAPHING
12. COORDINATION
13. FOCUS
14. POWER
15. TORQUE
16. BODY MOMENTUM
17. GRAVITATIONAL MARRIAGE
18. PENETRATION
19. TRANSITION
20. DISTANCE
21. COVER

"Kenpo is an evolution of opportunity,
           - that may only come once in combat"

CHAPTER 1

ERECT POSTURE

- Characteristic Way of Bearing One's Body -

It is one of the most basic things you are taught from childhood, stand up straight, have a strong back and erect posture, don't slouch. How someone carries himself or herself is an important part of life and is a very strong form of body language. If you stand up straight, it shows strength along with a positive attitude. People who have good posture also have a distinct **PRESENCE** about them. This is generated by poise, stature, and stateliness that distinguish them from the crowd. This type of body language almost always intimidates people due to the way in which a person holds themselves. It is one of the first basics that you will be taught in any

Kenpo school and for good reason. Having an erect straight posture puts your body in a neutral state as far as balance is concerned and allows you to move effortlessly from one move to the next. It allows you to have alternative **POSTURAL POSITIONS** for offensive as well as defensive techniques. Having a straight erect posture also has the added benefit of allowing you to assume a **POSITION OF READINESS**, this places you in the best possible position for techniques that might occur *before*, *during* or *after* combat starts.

Low roundhouse kick to the inside of the knee joint

I use this practically every day I work on the door. Many times people will square up to you that places you in a vulnerable dangerous position. Knowing when to realign your body in relation to someone who is standing in front of you in an aggressive manner is important, as training ingrains into your subconscious mind the realization and understanding of when to reposition yourself to the side or behind them. Applying this action will allow you to gain the best possible strategic position with which to defend yourself.

Having knowledge that your *action* or in some cases *inaction* will put you in a bad strategic position and that your posture and demeanor can affect how a situation unfolds, is fundamental to how you will apply your techniques. Placing your body in this state allows you greater ease of movement, which in turn will allow you to make a greater degree of directional change. This makes your use of motion for attacking and defense purposes much more effective.

Front thrust kick to the abdomen

Once you have placed yourself in a position of readiness, the use of an **ERECT POSTURE** is instrumental in promoting the use of peripheral vision, which is extremely important when dealing with more than one attacker. When you practice forms for example, you are taught to keep your hips in line with your shoulders as it promotes good balance whilst distributing your body weight evenly over both legs. If you also practice your self-defense techniques with a training partner, you will quickly realize that having a straight back places you in a **NEUTRAL POSITION** which enables you to adjust and realign your body with greater ease than if you were leaning over in one direction or another. It simply makes the practice of your **BASIC FUNDAMENTALS** more efficient and effective.

If you have bad posture this will show up as bad technique when you are practicing your drills or spar with your training partner. That is not to say that having a straight posture should be maintained indefinitely, it is a neutral position that allows you to access alternative postural positions used in combat. Whether this is executing a roundhouse kick, punch, lock, or applying techniques on the ground. The position of your upper body is relevant to the technique that you are executing. For example, if you were to throw a high round house kick to the head of your opponent the upper body acts as a pendulum for your action in counter balancing you're kicking leg with your body. As you lean back, it will accelerate the leg to your opponents head or upper body whilst at the same time moving your head and upper body away from a potential punch or kick.

What you will experience as you progress through the 21 priority principles is that one principle will automatically trigger another principle. They literally back each other up to become *one* overriding principle of motion. It is also important to understand that the principles of motion do not function independently of one-another and are not executed in isolation. If we miss with one strike, we can automatically continue into the next move of our technique sequence, thus ensuring we have a backup system of movements in place, as well as postural changes.

How does this translate into a self-defense situation on the street? Having a straight posture not only gives you the advantage of increased peripheral vision, but it is a neutral position from which to fight from. You are not committed to any action other than seeking neutrality in how you are standing and where your hand positions should be. If you have an understanding of how danger strikes then **ACCEPTANCE** should be at the top of your **SELF-DEFENSE CONSIDERATIONS**. Without acknowledging that a self-defense situation could happen at any time, you are leaving yourself open to becoming just another victim and national statistic.

CHAPTER 2

BALANCE

- The State of Equilibrium -

Depending on your perspective of life, balance can mean one of two things. Balance in your life in how you manage your time and what you do with it, or actual balance when referring to weight distribution. Both of these elements have relevance to your training in Kenpo. However, in this section, we are going to concentrate on the physical balance that is needed from your stances along with the overall balance of your body when fighting.

Roy Travert and Bob Lyles practicing punching

When executing a fighting technique, good balance is essential to your training if you are to generate and maintain power throughout the execution of your technique. It is a key ingredient in increasing your skill level in Kenpo and is enhanced by the addition of an **ERECT POSTURE**. To maintain good balance the body must be in a state of relaxation, tensing only at the moment of impact. The joints must be flexible and supple to ensure good balance when executing you're kicking, blocking, and punching techniques. Developing good balance will prevent you from over leaning with the possibility of you overextending your technique. Maintaining good balance that allows you to strike targets quickly and powerfully is a key factor in achieving proper weight distribution. You will find that stability in your stances will be far greater by distributing your body weight evenly and proportionately depending on the stance that you are using, along with the purpose it is intended for. Having good balance enables your body to be poised and ready for action. That is not to say that you will always be in the optimal position when actually fighting. Your opponent will try to destabilize this position to gain an advantage over you. If and when this happens, you must train to be able to reestablish a neutral balanced position as quickly as possible.

It is also important to practice techniques that require you to have **CONTACT MANIPULATION** in them, which includes techniques that are practiced on the ground. This is a very important part of your training as you must have a feeling of what it is like to actually grab someone whilst they resist what you are trying to do to them. Practicing your techniques in the air will add to your total fighting ability by adding **SPEED** to your hand and footwork, but the same techniques will feel totally different when you land them on the heavy bag or your training partner resists your action. Your **DEPTH OF PENETRATION** will change depending on the target you are striking, which is why it is so important to **"feel"** how this will affect your balance when making positional adjustments with your body. When you train, think about how having good balance affects your delivery of a specific technique. If for example you have to realign your footwork which requires that you "step up the circle," to gain a new **ANGLE OF ENTRY** to specific targets on your opponents body, having balance when you settle into your new stance is essential to the execution of the technique, thus preventing you falling over in the process of delivering it.

To achieve any amount of power in your strikes or blocks, you must have balance as you shift your body weight from one stance to the next. Without doing so will cause you to become unbalanced with the possibility of you going to the ground. Balance if applied correctly, will even produce stability when standing on one leg whilst executing a kick or punch regardless of your body positioning and posture. The only way to achieve good balance when training is to practice drills that develop this particular part of your training regime. Practicing your kicks whilst standing on one leg is a good way to start this process. You can start by shifting your weight from your neutral bow stance into a cat stance, from this position you simply lift your front leg so you are standing in a one-legged crane stance. Hold this position for a few seconds and see how your body weight feels. Slowly extend your front leg to full extension then slowly retrieve it back to its original position. If you practice this drill slowly, you will start to feel yourself compensating where your central body weight actually is, you will then start to realign it to your **CENTER LINE** in relation to the mass of your body whilst achieving good balance. This body state will lead you to **BALANCE COMPENSATION**. This is the continual adjustment of your body *before*, *during*, and *after* contact is made with an opponent. After you have learned enough basics to be able to add and subtract them in a logical working sequence, your training will progress to more structured components. Self-defense technique training gives you the framework to apply your principles whilst blocking or striking, they are an essential component in developing *balance in motion.*

Roy Travert and Jeff Speakman, practicing Triggered Salute

Not only should you practice to retain good balance whilst kicking, but also whilst you are in motion delivering any combination of empty hand techniques. This should be in **COORDINATION** with stances, footwork, and upper body strikes and blocks. These will include punching, hammer fists, hand swords, and heel palms. In fact, you can use any hand combination that relies on you delivering the strike whilst pivoting into any combination of stances. A forward bow stance will shift your weight forward adding **BACK UP MASS** behind the striking weapon. Dropping your body vertically will use the dimension of height to achieve **POWER** by using **MARRIAGE OF GRAVITY** to add **PENETRATION** to your strike, this is especially useful when your opponent is on the ground. Although we tend to view balance from our own point of view, it is also worth considering it from your opponent's point of view as well. Combat has many dimensions to it, the unbalancing of your opponent using a **STRIKE**, **SWEEP** or **TAKE-DOWN** should also be practiced as they are formidable weapons in your arsenal that enable you to drop your opponent to the ground. Using these techniques will give you the ability to put your opponent into a prone or reactionary position on the floor. Even then, you must still have good balance if you are to dominate and take advantage of this position.

Andrew Toporis and Fraser Bentley Sparring

Your priority when developing your skills in Kenpo is to have control of your **own** *height*, *width*, and *depth* zones **first**. If you have no control over your own dimensions, how can you expect to control your opponents? So make sure you spend enough time working out on the heavy punch bag, working on your balance and settling your body weight whilst moving. Making contact with a heavy object is not the same as developing your sparring or self-defense technique skills, which develop other technical aspects of your training. By enabling you to **FOCUS** on different **ANGLES** as well as the weapons employed to hit them, striking the heavy bag acts as a barometer as to how hard you can actually hit something along with the areas of your training that you will need to work on.

CHAPTER 3

RELAX

- Become Less Tense -

Learning to relax is an integral part of your training program which should not be overlooked. In Kenpo, we start our training sessions by dropping into a meditating horse stance, closing our eyes and clearing our mind of all outside thoughts. This practice allows you to concentrate on the lesson ahead whilst leaving any negative disruptive thoughts outside the Dojo. Having a structured process that teaches relaxation techniques as part of your general workout, is essential if you are to gain the most out of your training. Relaxation involves two parts, the *mental relaxation* you get from meditation and the **FOCUS** of your mind and the *physical relaxation* of training which involves stretching your body so that it functions with the minimal risk of injury and at its optimal physical level. This includes the practice of Kenpo as a physical form of exercise whilst learning self-defense skills, the overall effect is to improve your overall wellbeing and health.

MENTAL RELAXATION

Developing the ability to be relaxed when fighting takes perseverance and dedicated training. It takes time and patience to learn how to relax your mind and body to work as one effective fighting unit. Training under pressure with a good instructor will help you to react to various situations with precise focused technique. Having a relaxed focused mind will aid you in achieving this goal. Try to **FOCUS** your training into two parts when developing your relaxation techniques. Mental and physical relaxation.

The first part of your training should develop your ability to remain calm and relaxed under pressure. Having the ability to keep a clear focused calm mind whilst a physical or verbal confrontation takes place, takes training and practice. This can only be achieved through the practice of scenarios that place a greater amount of emphasis on this part of your training. Remaining calm whilst someone is shouting and swearing at you is a skill that takes time to develop. Most people will automatically retaliate when faced with a situation like this, with some form of verbal abuse aimed back at their aggressor. Unfortunately, this can inflame an already volatile situation into a physical confrontation. Your aim in a situation like this is a de-escalation of the confrontation, *not* an escalation into physical violence. Consistent training that develops your ability to remain calm under pressure is the key to mental relaxation. Remember, it takes a far greater person to walk away from a confrontation than to walk towards it.

PHYSICAL RELAXATION

Learning how to relax your body contributes to having **GOOD BALANCE** and can be achieved by stretching your limbs to become more flexible and supple. This, in turn, will increase your speed which will allow you to have much quicker reaction times when attacking an opponent or defending yourself against an attack. The benefits of stretching when training cannot be overemphasized, it will allow you to operate with greater **SPEED** and will increase your reaction times greatly. If you have trained correctly, you will be able to change the direction of your weapon or body at will, which will be accompanied with far greater speed and acceleration if your body is stretched, flexible, and relaxed.

This is transferred over into your martial arts training program by relaxing in-between strikes which will increase your physical speed and allow you to land your techniques with greater **POWER**. Relaxation is an essential primary ingredient of your skill base, without which your movements will be jerky and stiff. Relaxing has many residual benefits and certainly contributes to adding power to your strikes and blocks, it also aids in **FOCUSING** your mind on the present moment. All of which makes for a much more balanced focused fighter. Incorporating a structured training regime into your daily schedule that allows time to stretch and relax is just as important as a physical workout based on kicking and punching drills. Do not neglect this part of your training.

THE BENEFITS OF RELAXING

The residual effects of practicing relaxation techniques can be a marked improvement in your overall health, fitness, and wellbeing, whilst reducing the symptoms of stress-related illnesses by:

- Reducing your heart rate
- Lowering high blood pressure
- Slowing your breathing rate
- The reduction of cortisol, your body's stress hormone
- Improving blood flow to major muscles
- Reducing muscle tension and chronic pain
- Increase production of brain chemicals called endorphins
- Lowering fatigue and improving concentration

ACTIVE STRESS MANAGEMENT

Although this is a subdivision of relaxation, it is still worthy of a mention and should be incorporated as part of your overall training and development. The best way to manage any form of stress, which includes fighting and confrontation, is to learn healthy strategies that enable you to cope with any situation you may come across in life, not just when you're training in the Dojo.

RELAXATION TRAINING

You can start practicing the following strategies until you find specific ones that work for you. Everyone is different in how they respond to various elements of training. You should practice these techniques until you form new habits which will improve your concentration and general well-being.

1. **Meditate**
2. **Train often**
3. **Breathe correctly**
4. **Listen to your body**
5. **Be in the present moment**
6. **Be social**

Relaxation training combined with relaxation techniques are any method or activity that helps you to relax and attain a state of calmness. The development of this type of training involves both the physical application of circular breathing techniques, combined with psychological techniques such as meditation. This is especially important at the beginning and end of every Kenpo class where you are taught to clear your mind of all outside thoughts and concentrate on the lesson ahead of you. Each individual may find they benefit more from one element of training than another person does. Relaxation training can also help reduce increased levels of pain derived from increased physical activity, another by-product of training in Kenpo can be the reduction of anxiety whilst controlling stress and improving anger management issues.

1. MEDITATE

A few minutes of practice each day can help ease stress levels and reduce anxiety. In Kenpo, we start each training session by dropping into a meditating horse stance, with our left open hand over our right clenched fist. We continue by closing our eyes and bowing our head slightly. Slowly breathe in through the nose and out through the mouth. Repeat this several times and relax your shoulders when you exhale. Start to concentrate your mind on what you intend to do in the lesson and do not let anything distract you. This technique can also be used during your normal working day, even if you're stressed out at work these techniques will help you remain calm and focused. Just find somewhere you can sit down for a few minutes and carry out the breathing exercise. Sit up with your back straight with both of your feet flat on the floor. Close your eyes and start to **FOCUS** on what you would like to achieve throughout the day. You could even recite the Kenpo Creed in your mind to give you something positive to concentrate on. The creed will help develop a positive mental attitude towards life and a healthy lifestyle. It is a code to live life from.

KENPO CREED

"I come to you with only Karate, empty hands. I have no weapons, but should I be forced to defend myself, my principles, or my honor, should it be a matter of life or death, of right or wrong; then here are my weapons, Karate, my empty hands"

Ed Parker

2. TRAIN OFTEN

All forms of exercise, including Kenpo, yoga, and walking, can have huge health benefits by easing depression and anxiety with the release of feel-good chemicals called endorphins. Endorphins are released into the body by the pituitary gland located at the base of the brain. They are then distributed throughout the body via the central nervous system. The principal function of endorphins is to inhibit the transmission of pain signals, exercise helps your body stay fit and healthy, with the release of endorphins adding to your feeling of well-being and euphoria before, during, and after training.

All of which helps you to relax. How many times after having a workout have you gone home and said to yourself **"wow I feel great!"** that is the natural opioid effect of the endorphins traveling through your body. You do not need to engage in hard physical activity to achieve this state either, any form of physical activity will achieve the desired result. Simply going for a quick walk, taking the stairs instead of using the lift, or doing some stretching exercises will all help you to relax and feel good about yourself.

You don't have to run a marathon in order to get a runner's high, you simply need to do some form of exercise that releases endorphins into your body. Even if you spend 15 minutes a day training one individual aspect of Kenpo you will feel good about yourself. Kenpo is a lifelong study of motion that should be practiced every day of your life. Remember you are only as good as your last training session, so make sure you train regularly.

3. BREATHE CORRECTLY

If you have been training in the martial arts for any length of time, or if you are a beginner, you will have been taught the value of breathing correctly to generate power in your strikes, and how to fortify your body whilst doing so. In Kenpo, we are taught to use a circular breathing method that entails breathing in through the nose and out through the mouth. Although there are certain exceptions to this rule.

This extremely effective method allows you to fill your lungs to full capacity whilst exhaling out through the mouth with a sharp explosive action. This is very useful to generate power whilst striking or blocking when used in conjunction with the Kiai (気合), /'kiː.aɪ/ is a Japanese term used in martial arts for the short yell or shout uttered when performing an attacking move.

However, you can also use this breathing method to relax. Take a 5-minute break and focus on your breath control. Sit up straight, eyes closed. Slowly inhale through your nose, feeling the breath start in your abdomen and work its way to the top of your head. Reverse the process as you exhale through your mouth.

Deep breathing counters the effects of stress by slowing the heart rate and lowering blood pressure, a word of caution, the object of using the correct technique is not to flood your body with oxygen leading to a state of hyperventilation. If used correctly it will enable you to function under stress in a combat situation by being as relaxed as possible but with a highly focused functional mindset.

TRAINING TIP:

DO NOT HOLD YOUR BREATH

Although breathing correctly will help you to relax, a common mistake that a student will make is to hold their breath when either training or fighting. Making sure you exhale when you hit something is one of the most important aspects of your training. You must resist the temptation to hold your breath. This is extremely common and should be avoided at all costs. By holding your breath, you will sap your body of much-needed energy extremely quickly. It would be the equivalent of leaving the lights on your car as you watched the battery drain flat.

Many fights are lost not because the practitioner was not skilled enough, but because they did not synchronize their breathing with their blocks and strikes, they then simply ran out of energy to keep fighting. Training with a partner will prevent this from happening by pushing yourself to the boundaries of your physical fitness and skill base, you must then push past this point to get to another higher level of physical and mental fitness in your training. Training to become a fitter stronger fighter, should be at the very foundation of your training regime. Make sure you spend enough time hitting the heavy punch bag as this will allow you to synchronize your breathing at the exact moment you land a punch. Incorporate into your training schedule the development of three 3 minute rounds with a 30 second rest period in-between. This will increase your stamina whilst improving your overall fitness.

4. LISTEN TO YOUR BODY

The martial arts are a fantastic form of physical activity that not only allows you to build a strong body but also a strong mental mindset as well. It is so complex and multi-layered that it can take over your life, literally. If you are like me and if you ever missed a training session because of work commitments, injury, or because you were simply burned out, you would be racked with guilt and would train twice as hard the following session. The truth however, is that missing one or two training sessions will not make any difference to your studies of Kenpo or any martial art for that matter. Learning to listen to how your body feels is extremely important if you are to progress your studies and increase your knowledge base.

Over-training without resting will hamper your overall progress and limit your gains. Training in any form of combat system is physically demanding and you will pick up small niggling injuries that can accumulate over a long period of time. This will inevitably hamper your long-term progress and development in Kenpo if not addressed and resolved. You cannot train to the level that we do in Kenpo and not pick up injuries, you have to be realistic, if you are training with people who are throwing punches and kicks at you then at some point you are going to get hit!

I have had some serious injuries over the years, the most severe happened when I was in my twenties, an instructor I was learning a technique from ruptured my L4 and L5 (Lumber) discs in my spine. Never having had an injury like this before, I thought I could just train through it. That was my first mistake, the pain from an injury like this is debilitating to the point that you never think you will recover from it or train properly again. After attending numerous sessions with a chiropractic consultant and having cortisone injections in my spine, I started to research about this particular injury and how I could follow a structured rehabilitation program that would enable me to get back to training. During this period, I learned a great deal about how the body worked and what I needed to do to repair it. A lot of positives came out of a negative situation.

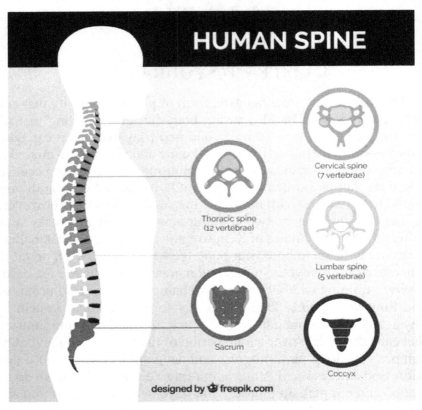

At one particular point in my recovery, I had a serious setback, the specialist who was treating me suggested that I have my spine fused and plates inserted to support the lower back, this would have effectively ended my training in Kenpo. Needless to say, I refused to have this done, I was only 22 at the time and knew I had a lifetime to recover from the injury and get stronger again. I started to learn new stretching techniques that would strengthen and support the muscles around the injury and after an enforced period of rest, I returned back to a class environment. I did this in a slow methodical way that enabled me to build strength in my posture and get the muscles in my lower back used to working again. I slowly practiced forms at the rear of the class until I reached a point in my training that I could participate in the main workout again. Although this was a severe injury that literally stopped me in my tracks, thirty years on from it, I am still training nearly every day.

I am telling you this story, to make sure you do not make the same mistakes as I did in trying to keep on training when the reality was I should have been resting and listening to my body. It simply needed time for the swelling and inflammation to calm down and for the muscle and ligament damage to have time to repair itself. Trying to train through this type of injury is counterproductive and will not allow the body to repair itself successfully.

"Mistakes are only good,
* - if you recognize them and learn from them"*

The upside of an injury like this (if there is one) is that it prompted me to change the way in which I trained. I started to consult with other fitness professionals on alternative methods of stretching that I could incorporate into my Kenpo classes. The result was that I slowly started to recover from a life-changing injury that could have ended my study of Kenpo. Instead, I used it as a positive and trained in alternative aspects of the art whilst spending time developing stretching techniques, form training, and pad work. All these aspects of training would eventually make my body strong again. Interestingly, all of these elements combined helped increase my knowledge of Kenpo by studying areas of the art that may otherwise have been neglected.

The moral of this story is that it is a lot easier to learn by other people's mistakes, if you need to take time out from training because of work commitments, family commitments, or injury then do so. Don't miss out on your life of what's truly important and don't be afraid to slow down and listen to your body to enable you to recover and relax a little. Learning to relax whilst fighting takes training and focus, however, the end result will be a much more balanced and productive training regime with rest incorporated into it as an essential part of your training.

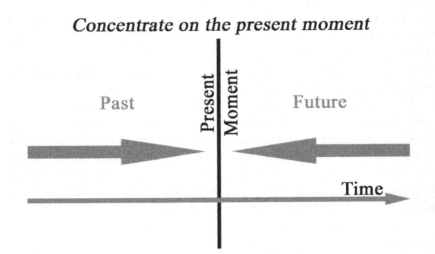

Concentrate on the present moment

Past　　Present Moment　　Future

Time

5. BE IN THE PRESENT MOMENT

Life is in a constant state of change and unfolds in the present, not the past or future. Kenpo is a dynamic form of martial art, training in it is exciting, and physically challenging, learning self-defense techniques and freestyle fighting combinations take up a considerable amount of time. Much of your training is geared towards the next grading or a competition fight in a couple of months' time. Training in this way does not allow you to spend time on what you have already learned and in many cases adds a subtle layer of stress to your training. This is normal, but you must also spend time focusing on the now, focusing on the syllabus that you have already learned and the value that it brings to your overall study of Kenpo. It is good to set yourself short, medium, and long-term goals, but they should not add stress to your overall training structure.

Having a relaxed focused attitude to training, allows you to concentrate on what is important and what is not. There is no point in worrying about something if it hasn't happened yet, far too many people focus on the "What if" in life, as well as the "What if" in a self-defense technique, instead of focusing on the moment they are actually in. People dwell on what happened in the past and worry about what could happen in the future. Both of these mindsets are distractions to you focusing on the present moment, the here, and now. This translates over into your training by developing your skill set at incremental levels. Focusing on a particular part of your training and compartmentalizing it into individual components allows you to refine and master a particular move at a much greater rate. The development of a mindset that concentrates on the moment you are actually training, is necessary to achieve this. If for example, someone is trying to punch you in the face and you simply stand in the same position without reacting to it, your state of mind is in a state of denial. You think that the situation isn't actually happening and that you are imagining it. Unfortunately, your mind can deceive you into thinking that everyone is nice, kind, and good-hearted when the reality is most people would rob you for a dime.

Self-protection starts in your mind, it is aided by the introduction of physical techniques that you can use to protect yourself. Learn to kick the bag hard and concentrate your mind on that part of your training session, be in the present and **do not** worry about how you performed last week, or how you might kick in the future. Concentrate on that training session on that particular day and strive to improve your technique for the next session. When entering the Dojo you must clear your mind of all outside thoughts, this is practiced at the beginning and end of every training session. This is important as you need to develop an active, open state of awareness that is focused on the present.

This transfers over into your training session by focusing your mind on the drill or technique you are presently learning. Do not get stressed or frustrated if you have difficulty when learning something new. Everything in life takes time to learn and it all starts with the first step. Coupled with the fact that people are very different and will all favor one technique application over another, try to focus on what you are learning at that particular point in time.

Slow your training down and take 5 minutes to focus on only one behavior but do it with awareness. Drill the application until you are sick of it, this is the only way to achieve spontaneous reaction when you are in a confrontation. When you spend time in the moment and focus on your senses, which includes your breathing, sight, and hearing, you should feel less tense and become more aware of what is going on around you. This will enhance your overall **ENVIRONMENTAL AWARENESS** and your ability to sense danger.

Roy Travert and Mr. Frank Trejo at Bryan Hawkins training camp Los Angeles

6. BE SOCIAL

As this is a subsection of active stress management, in certain circumstances it can be beneficial to use your social network at your Dojo to handle stress and discuss matters in private with your instructor. Stress can come from many different areas of your life including training in Kenpo. One of your best tools for handling stress and dealing with any problems you might have is to have face to face communication with people and talk to others about any issue you might have. Believe it or not, but your martial arts school and organization is a huge social hub, so use it to make new friends and integrate into classes. Attending seminars and training with other people that share similar ideas and experiences, is fundamental in creating a social community that encourages the development of ethical, moral and social codes of conduct. Above all, do not talk about people behind their backs, any issues that you may have should be discussed in private away from any group view.

Fighting is stressful, it is how you handle the stress from any form of confrontation that is important to your overall well-being and personal development. We all lead very hectic busy lives, with many people training in Kenpo to relieve some of that stress. Any form of physical activity is a great tool for releasing feel-good endorphins into your body. Communication skills are just as important to learn when training in Kenpo as the actual physical application of fighting techniques. The requirements for progression to black belt include your ability to teach and pass on the knowledge you have already learned to new students. This helps to develop key social skills through close interaction with other people whilst developing your ability to teach. It has to be said that not everyone will enjoy or even wish to take part in this particular part of their studies. Some people are great fighters but not great teachers. Some people are great teachers but not great fighters. Your aim is to become the best you can be at both, a great fighter and an ambassador for the art. Simply aim to be the best you can be.

CHARACTER BUILDING

Mr. Parker developed the Kenpo Creed to lay the foundations of a moral training structure in Kenpo. The creed is extended at every belt level to instill character-building qualities in the individual learning the Kenpo system. It is hoped that by having a moral code of conduct that is in sync with the physical fighting skills that comes from training, it will produce balance in an individual's character that is not attainable through physical performance and development alone. To emphasize this character development and state of mind, the following pledge is from Mr. Parker's Kenpo extended creed:

2nd Brown Belt Pledge

I understand that like a doctor, the private affairs of students and fellow instructors that come to my attention during the exercising of my responsibilities are privileged communications and must never be discussed with any living soul. I vow that I will never violate this pledge or any other for the sake of personal benefit.

"Kenpo is a system of fighting,
   - that allows the individual to develop their own style"

CHAPTER 4

SPEED

- Move Fast -

Speed is an important contributing factor to **POWER**, it is literally skill combined with accuracy, and takes precedence over the application of power. Although it should be considered a *primary principle* when applying your techniques, it should also be used with accuracy. Failing to do so would render the use of speed as useless or wasted motion. Having said that, you should always be fast when striking with any weapon, making sure you retrieve and re-chamber it for a secondary strike immediately after you have thrown your initial technique. Failing to do so will give your opponent the opportunity to counter your initial offensive move. This could entail the grabbing and restraining of your weapon with the potential to take you to the ground with a sweep or take-down.

Always be sharp and crisp when executing your strikes and **never** leave a weapon hanging out for an opponent to grab. It is never wise in combat to gift your opponent a free sweep by leaving your slow kick hanging out for them to grab, or when you shoot in low for a take-down but end up with a knee in the face in the process because you were too slow to grab your assailants leg, or execute an effective block. Although I have covered this particular subject in my first book Kenpo - How to Survive Life, it is one of the most important principles that you need to apply when fighting. The practical application of applying this valuable principle cannot be overemphasized when you are actually fighting.

SPEED A BASIC PRINCIPLE

The application of speed as a whole is divided into three parts:

- Perceptual Speed
- Mental Speed
- Physical Speed

PERCEPTUAL SPEED – VISUAL THINKING

The technical terminology for speed is the ability to rapidly compare visual configurations and information with the potential to identify some particular detail that is buried in distracting material. Visual thinking can also be used to compare objects, numbers, letters, or patterns. Now that might sound complicated to a lot of people, but in simple terms, it really means that it's your ability to see the type of attack coming towards you and how you react to it. One of the primary mental abilities in visual thinking is *perceptual speed*. Motion has defined paths or lines of action that you or your opponent's weapons can travel on. By developing perceptual speed you will be able to recognize whether it is going to be a straight line attack such as front jab or reverse punch, or a circular technique such as roundhouse kick or punch such as an uppercut or hook. This same principle is also applied to kicking techniques. When we train in

Kenpo, we will use specifically defined ways of moving that are used consistently to produce the desired result in combat. We will use various patterns of motion that may be used at the same time or one after the other. These are "Key Movements" such as lines and circles that you or your opponent can use. It is your ability to react to this information and have the capability to process it quickly and accurately in your brain that is essential to your training.

This is particularly important during periods of *stress* and *pressure* when involved in a fight. Perceptual speed relies on the quickness of the senses. The stimulus for this type of speed may come from your sight, hearing, smell, or touch. With this newly acquired information, it is then relayed to the brain for analysis, once this is processed it is then down to your skill level and ability to make the correct decision in applying your technique to any given situation. To increase this type of speed, conditioning of the senses is necessary. Practicing mental drills that increase your ability to monitor a situation before reacting to it, is very useful when faced with any type of confrontation.

BODY LANGUAGE

This nonverbal method of communication involves body movement or gestures. People can convey a great deal of communication without actually speaking. This is one method that we already use to increase our awareness of our environment and the people that are in it. When you are out and about, take some time to sit and watch the mannerisms of people around you and how they interact with other people, which also includes yourself. Are people overly aggressive when you speak to them? Are they compliant with what you are saying to them? Do they have their own opinion on certain matters? Learning about **BODY LANGUAGE** and how it can affect the speed at which you react to an attack or verbal confrontation, is an often overlooked subdivision of your training. I have worked as security in nightclubs for years, and it is essential that you develop your skills in reading a situation before it escalates to the point that physical intervention is required. Although this is not always practical or preventable. Talking first in trying to defuse a situation should be your first priority. Maintaining and having a working respect for *environmental awareness* is an important part of this subsection of speed. Having the ability to recognize that a situation is developing, and then take the necessary action before it hits its critical mass, is just as important as having the ability to react to it if it is already in full motion.

PEOPLE WATCHING

The most important part of my job is to stand and watch people. That is the job I am paid to do. Sometimes it is extremely boring and sometimes it is extremely violent. Nevertheless, the information you can gain by watching people and how a person's demeanor can draw your attention to them before a fight breaks out is a critical part of your training. Do not walk around with blinkers on! Pay attention at all times to your environment and who is in it, observe what they are doing and whether it will pose a threat to you, your friends, or your family. This is especially important if you are out socializing in a nightclub. With some venues holding hundreds if not thousands of people, having your wits about you is very important. Not everybody is going out to have fun, with the intention to meet people and enjoy themselves, a small minority will be getting extremely drunk taking drugs and looking for trouble. This is where the old saying "prevention is always better than a cure," is relevant to situations like this. Which is why it is always a good idea to not only learn physical techniques to kick, punch and restrain with, but also develop the ability to read a situation through the use of body language. This is an important use of psychology being used as a weapon in fighting, the study of which has been documented extensively over the years. However, it is still important to your overall development as a Kenpo practitioner to study the effects of it in a real-world situation that is relevant to the streets.

Whenever I have had to make a statement to the police in relation to any incidents we have had in the club, I have always emphasized the body language and mannerisms of the person or persons involved. Some points to consider that may help you if you ever need to make a statement of your own are:

- Were they overly aggressive towards you
- What type of clothes were they wearing
- Did they have any distinguishing marks, such as tattoos
- Did they step towards you in an aggressive manner
- Did they throw the first strike
- Were they verbally abusive to you first
- Were you recorded on CCTV, this can be used as evidence

Through my own experiences and that of my work colleagues, some of these points could prove to be very important if legal proceedings were ever instigated and the case brought before a court of law. This leads us into another subdivision of people watching, which can be divided into four divisions of its own. You will find them to be useful to your studies when you are out and about socially, this is an often overlooked aspect of your training.

They consist of the following categories:

- **IDENTITY**
- **SELF ESTEEM**
- **EMOTIONAL STATE**
- **EXTROVERSION**

IDENTITY

People like to identify with something or someone, and if you watch people for long enough you will see a trend developing with what they are wearing and who they like to be associated with. This could be a particular type of jacket that shows they are a member of a sailing club or a baseball cap that states the team they support. This is no different to wearing a Kenpo jacket or school uniform in the Dojo. Everyone who wears a piece of sports regalia or uniform is telling the people around them about the region, college, or nation with which they wish to identify and belong to. This also applies to the less desirable elements of society.

People don't actually have to be from that place, but by dressing themselves in this way they are making a statement to the people around them, and to the world that this is the image they wish to convey of themselves. This includes where they come from, and with whom they wish to associate themselves. This also extends to people who wear designer logos to show that they wish to appear affluent and fashionable.

People also show their identity in the travel souvenirs they wear. When they decide to carry around handbags that have the message "New York" or "Los Angeles", they send out the message to others that they are world travelers, sophisticated, and cosmopolitan. Having a Tattoo is another clue to a person's identity. A tattoo is a permanent alteration of the body to show what each person values along with what and who they identify with. All these elements allow you to gather information about people. However, you must never judge a person on how they look, the old saying that you should "Never judge a book by its cover" is true of people watching, and how they wish to identify themselves in society. Thieves, crooks, liars, and rapists do not go about society advertising the fact that they are who they are. They tend to blend in to become inconspicuous, as I have stated before, never trust anyone until they prove themselves to be trustworthy.

SELF ESTEEM

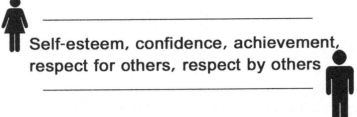

Self-esteem, confidence, achievement, respect for others, respect by others

In psychology and sociology, self-esteem reflects a person's overall subjective emotional evaluation of his or her own worth and self. It is a judgment of oneself as well as an attitude toward the *self,* it is generally the way in which people carry themselves that communicates the esteem with which they personally hold themselves in.

A person who has a good posture, with their shoulders pushed back and head held high, combined with a confident walk and gait, communicates that they feel strong and secure about themselves. However, it is possible to go too far with this type of body language to a point that people can convey a sense of arrogance, rather than confidence when they hold themselves in such high regard that they look down on others. This can be especially true in the world of martial arts, so train to keep your ego in check and be respectful of others when training in the Dojo, and even more so when out on the street.

Conversely, people who have a bad posture are telling the world that they are beset with feelings of insecurity and self-doubt. This type of body language is often the focus of fraudsters, con men, and manipulators who are looking for a vulnerable easy soft target to exploit. Be wary of anything that is **"free"** and **"too good to be true"**, it is normally a con and should be avoided at all cost. People who give out the vibe that they are vulnerable, are easily exploited by fraudsters who are experts in identifying individuals to manipulate. It is hoped, that by training in Kenpo, you will build your confidence levels to such a degree that you will be able to deal with stressful situations like this, and become aware of the type of people that would otherwise take advantage of you.

EMOTIONAL STATE

> **"You might be in a person's life,**
> **- but you are not in their head"**

The emotional state of someone is an unknown entity, it is something that is not visible to the naked eye which makes it even harder to anticipate their intended action. Outwardly, they may look perfectly normal but you simply have no idea what they are thinking, and whether they are rational or not. There can be a tendency when practicing self-defense techniques to totally disregard the emotional state of an opponent and whether this might have a negative effect on the outcome in protecting yourself.

Arm yourself with the knowledge that the person who has nothing in life has nothing to lose. They are the most dangerous people in society as they have no compassion for mankind or abide by the same rules that society accepts as normal behavior. You must be mindful that this type of person is like a chameleon, they can blend into society without arousing suspicion which makes them extremely difficult to spot, only showing their true colors when forced to do so. Rightly or wrongly, one of the most important judgments we make about other people is normally based on their appearance and how they behave. A person's emotional state cannot only be seen in their body language but in their facial expressions as well. You can gauge their feelings not just by what they say to you when you speak to them, but from their stance, the way in which they walk, and the way in which they use their hands.

Anxious people tend to fidget a lot, dart their head from side to side and shrug their shoulders, which generally shows they are tense. They may even open and close their hands into fists whilst they talk to you without actually realizing it. Depression may also reveal itself in a sad facial expression but again, if you're not close enough to see, you can gauge this emotional state from a slowed-down pace of walking with their head dropped forward. When you're depressed, you don't feel like moving very quickly, and this is reflected in a person's gait and how they walk. If you walk around with blinkers on you will miss all these telltale signs of a person's emotional state.

Conversely, people who are happy walk more briskly, they may even have a little bit of a skip in their step and do not generally want to attack anyone for no reason. In addition to these telltale signs of someone's emotional state, they may continually tug at their purse or briefcase, or hold it in front of their bodies as a symbol that they seek to protect themselves from harm. Never underestimate the level someone will go to when threatened, in a time of extreme stress, they may consider using any available object as a weapon.

In today's modern society stress can be a huge mitigating factor in a person's emotional state and whether they have a stable personality or not. This is something you will have no knowledge of if and when you witness someone having an emotional episode. Unless the person who is shouting and screaming at the ticket attendant tells you, that they are in fact having a nervous breakdown you will not have the necessary information to make a judgment call. In most cases, this will not happen.

Money problems, marital breakdowns, and worries about job security can all put someone under extreme emotional pressure that is then vented in one form or another on the general population. People start behaving in a way that they wouldn't normally do and do things that are out of character for them. This can include drinking heavily, drug misuse, which includes painkillers, and the taking of anti-depressants. It may also lead to a violent episode if not dealt with professionally. Always consider if you are ever involved in a confrontation that there may be mitigating circumstances that you are not aware of and should treat all such incidents with extreme caution.

EXTROVERSION

Being an extrovert is not a bad thing, it allows you to make friends easily. An extrovert is always ready to engage others in conversation and seeks stimulation from their environment. They can be spotted in any gathering as the ones who make eye contact or initiate conversation with all who pass near them. Rather than retreating into the corner, they know how to "work the crowd." Whether at a party or in a waiting room. You get the feeling that the extrovert is always ready to shake someone's hand, whether it's offered to them or not.

You can also tell an extrovert by the type of clothes they wear, they will be the kind of person who dresses in the brightest colors. Although people often have a black day in which they purposefully select clothes to match their moods and their emotional state, extroverts are more likely to wear their personality literally on their sleeve using intense colors that proclaim their presence to all. This also relates to the martial artist who seeks acceptance and recognition by competing and winning tournaments. It is the acknowledgment of achieving something special and important that they seek.

EXTROVERTS TAKE RISKS

Extroverts live a life of risk and reward, thanks to their sensitivity to dopamine, a neurotransmitter that controls the brain's reward systems. When neurologists looked at the inner workings of extroverts' brains while they were in the process of gambling and winning, they found a spike of dopamine in the amygdala and the nucleus accumbens, these are two areas of the brain that are stimulated by external stimuli. Embracing risk isn't always a good thing, but it has its advantages. By not taking a risk sometimes, we run a bigger risk of being left behind.

EXTROVERTS THINK QUICKLY

Having the ability to think on your feet and to act fast when a dangerous situation presents itself is fundamental to your martial arts training. Fortunately, this state of mind can be developed and is especially important when training, it is an integral part of your *mental development to increase speed.* It is your ability to see two or three moves ahead of how the fight will unfold when you are applying your techniques at speed. This is normally done in a predetermined order that you have practiced in the Dojo to become spontaneous in any given situation.

A GAME OF CHESS

It's a bit like a chess player who is always looking at the long game, making a move that gives them the long-term advantage that will give them the ability to gain the dominant position and win the game. One wrong move however and the game can swing in your opponent's favor. This state of mind is not because extroverts are smarter or more intelligent than introverts, it's simply because their brains are wired slightly different. If you are training and you are a bit shy, developing a bit more extroversion is not a bad thing, getting out on the mat to do forms in front of your class can be a nerve-racking experience. It is, however, a great tool to use in your own personal development of this personality trait. Extroverts thrive on stimuli such as a new experience or an impromptu question from the boss, even if you feel uncomfortable exposing yourself to new experiences that take you out of your comfort zone, with perseverance you can expand your personality and acquire some of the positive aspects that this type of personality trait brings.

MENTAL SPEED – COGNITIVE ABILITY

The ability to process information at speed is at the basis of the cognitive process. It is one of the most important skills that a martial artist can have. Even if you do not possess these skills at the start of your training in Kenpo, you can learn them through the practice of basics and techniques. **Mental speed** is the quickness of the mind and its ability to relay newly acquired information collected from your senses to your limbs. Thus enabling you to make an effective response to any given situation based on predetermined movement patterns from your basics and various Kenpo techniques. These will have been practiced to the point that they have been internalized into your subconscious mind and are able to be used with spontaneous action. This will ultimately aid you in creating an instinctive effective response based on Kenpo techniques and movement patterns. Once again, do not isolate this type of speed in your fighting alone. Learn to *"read"* any situation and make moves to prevent something happening to you before it is too late. This includes walking in the opposite direction to a possible confrontation. Always consider that all options are available to you in circumventing a conflict or assault. Remain calm and walk away.

Walk away
from a confrontation

PHYSICAL SPEED

THE ABILITY TO MOVE QUICKLY

DISTANCE TRAVELED PER UNIT OF TIME

In simple terms, speed is the distance traveled per unit of time. It is how fast an object is moving. Speed is the scalar quantity that is the magnitude of the velocity vector. It doesn't have a direction.

- A higher speed means an object (including a limb) is moving faster.

- A lower speed means it is moving slower. If it isn't moving at all, it has zero speed.

Physical speed is the promptness of physical action. It is the application of basics and techniques that make up this type of speed. You can increase this subsection of speed in various ways, simply stretching will help to increase your range of movement and the speed you can throw a kick or punch at. If you are stiff or injured in some way, your ability to be fast will be diminished accordingly. **Body conditioning** is also an important factor to consider when developing this type of speed, as a fit healthy body will allow you to operate over long periods of time with the greatest effect. Speed must also be accompanied with **ACCURACY** if it is to be applied effectively. There is simply no point in throwing a punch if it is too far away from its target that it doesn't make contact, or it misses it altogether and goes past its target. When you practice techniques, they are the tools that allow you to develop these priority principles.

CHAPTER 5

ACCURACY

- The State or Degree of Being Precise -

As I have previously stated, there is absolutely no point in throwing a punch at someone if you miss your intended target. I have seen so many fights where the guys trying to punch each other, were so far away from hitting their targets that they may as well have sent each other a postcard telling them it was coming. One of the most common mistakes that people make when striking, is the **TELEGRAPHING** of their moves. Instead of moving the weapon, strike, or block from its point of origin, it is chambered back away from its target in the opposite direction. This is ok to do once you have rendered your opponent into a *prone position* and have sufficient time to do so, but you risk exposing yourself to a counter attack if you do not accompany your strike with speed and **ACCURACY** at the same time as you execute your technique.

Using a non-body contact method of countering to hide the strike

You need to disguise your moves as much as possible if you are to use the element of surprise to beat your opponent, especially if they have some fighting skills of their own. They may even see your strike chamber back before it even has a chance of being delivered. If this happens, it may enable them to move out of the way much more quickly or initiate a counter of their own. However, if the move was disguised by using a **DECEPTIVE MANEUVER** or originates from a **ZONE OF OBSCURITY** prior to executing the technique, the chances of success are greatly increased. Once again, it is perfectly ok to chamber a weapon back to generate more power when you are in a position to do so, but your initial move should be executed with **SPEED** and **ACCURACY** that strikes a **VITAL TARGET** (See: Kenpo – How to Survive Life) without telegraphing your move first. You can chamber your weapon back as much as you like when your opponent has been rendered into a *prone* or *reactionary* position that prevents them from hitting you back. Not only is it important to be accurate when executing your strikes, but it is just as important when using defensive techniques that **EVADE**, **BLOCK**, or **REDIRECT** an opponent's attack. Do not neglect the defensive aspect of your training which must also have the principle of accuracy applied to it. It goes without saying that it is just as important to use accuracy when using defensive techniques, as it is when using offensive techniques.

Developing accuracy as part of your skill set can be achieved a number of ways, start by practicing the technique in the air first, this could be a simple punching combination that incorporates a back fist, a rear cross, and an uppercut punch. Once you have practiced it to the point that you do not need to think about the sequence, or the targets you are striking, start to practice with a training partner. Start slowly so that you touch targets lightly. **DO NOT USE POWER AT THIS STAGE**. Once you have allowed for different body types and the **ANGLES** that are needed to gain access to targets, start to increase the **SPEED** of your movements. As we have already covered speed in the previous chapter, it is prudent to say that it is essential to use control when striking to vital targets. In many cases, you will experience your accuracy diminish as your speed increases. This is perfectly normal as your senses re-adjust your perceptual, mental, and physical abilities. Your goal is to be able to move at **SPEED** and hit your target with **POWER and ACCURACY**. Both of these principles should be applied to everything you do in Kenpo.

MULTIPLE STRIKES VERSUS SINGLE STRIKES

Fighting involves distinct methods of execution, with some being more effective than others. In many cases, some methods are more successful than others, some street brawlers may use the multiple haymaker approach where they will throw continuous punches in a wild uncontrolled manner, desperate in the hope that one will connect with their target. Most of the time this is done without being accurate or any consideration is given to the target it is aimed at. This uses a lot of energy and can lead to exhaustion very quickly.

The alternative method is to be accurate with one punch rather than many. It is much more energy efficient with a minimal waste of power, with the person preferring to throw one punch that connects to its target to get the job done. Both methods can be successful depending on the situation they are used in and how they are applied by the person using them. When training your aim is to use a combination of them **both** so that your use of offensive or defensive techniques are accurate and hit the target they are aimed at, using **SPEED** and **POWER**. Many times, I will see students practicing techniques with a partner and instead of aiming the strike at the target it is intended for, they will execute the strike past it, thus changing the *depth of penetration* and the accuracy of the technique. We do not teach our students to *pull* a punch in Kenpo, we teach them to *control* the punch or strike. In this way, they learn to focus on being accurate, whilst developing the ability to control the amount of power they use when hitting vital targets. This develops a greater understanding of the potential injury that can be caused by different weapons and the targets that are struck.

TRAINING POINT:

When you practice a technique, make sure you use control when practicing with your training partner, as it is essential for both of you to develop **accuracy** and **control** at the same time.

TRAINING EQUIPMENT:
THE HEAVY BAG

You can also work out on the heavy bag to develop the **POWER** aspect of your training. If there is one area of training that I enjoy the most, it's hitting the heavy bag. This is where you can *mentally visualize* the targets you are hitting, whilst developing accuracy in your skill set. This is an extremely useful piece of training equipment as it allows you to bring into play all elements of your training whilst hitting the bag with power. Not only will you develop accuracy training in this way, but it will quickly show any weakness in your **BODY ALIGNMENT** and technique delivery. Striking specific points on the bag whilst moving at speed requires you to concentrate as it is an essential aid in developing your accuracy whilst hitting a semi-solid object. It will not only improve the delivery of your kicking and punching techniques but will increase your overall accuracy, and improve your concentration levels. Using this method of training will require you to **locate** (perceptual speed), **react** (physical speed), and **respond** (mental speed) allowing you to become much more accurate in applying your technique. Again, start slowly and gradually increase the speed at which you execute your technique. However, as with all things to do with training, this isn't accomplished in one day, it takes many hours of repeating the same move over and over again with the completion of kicking and punching drills, to become proficient and accurate whilst moving at speed.

FOCUS MITTS

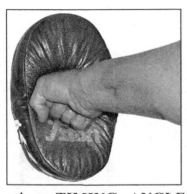

You can also practice with your training partner using focus mitts, this is a great way to develop accuracy using a much smaller target. Focus mitts are about the same size as a person's head, so make sure, when you hit them you aim for the center of the pad, not the outer edges. Training on the focus mitts should develop not only accuracy, but other key principles such as **TIMING**, **ANGLES**, and **COORDINATION** as well. Develop techniques that include punching combinations that **FLOW** into kicks than to elbows and then knee strikes. It is so important that you utilize and use all the ranges that combat covers. You must be able to hit targets using close-range weapons as well as long-range weapons. Regardless of the dimension or range being used, accuracy must be applied consistently to be effective.

Accuracy is critical when involved in a fight, I have seen some technically brilliant punches thrown that did not hit the target they were intended for. I have also seen people throw one punch that knocked the guy clean out. Accuracy is the key factor. There are literally hundreds of different methods that will help develop accuracy with your punching and kicking skills. Practicing drills, self-defense techniques, and sparring will all add to your overall growth in Kenpo and help develop this aspect of your training.

PRONE OR REACTIONARY POSITIONS

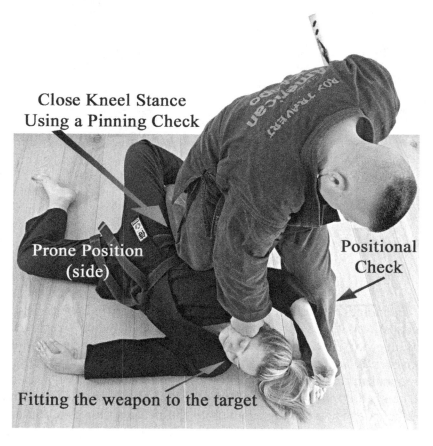

Close Kneel Stance
Using a Pinning Check

Prone Position
(side)

Positional
Check

Fitting the weapon to the target

An often overlooked aspect of fighting is the prone or reactionary positions that you are your opponent may end up in during combat. These positions can be the result of a strike, block, or maneuver that renders you or your opponent into a perilous or unstable position.

They can include positions that are:

- **Standing**
- **Partially standing**
- **Partially on the ground**
- **On the ground**

The practice of self-defense techniques requires that you consider the positions that your opponent can end up in when struck in a certain way. The principle of **ACCURACY** must be applied consistently for this to happen. If for example, you were to kick your opponent in the groin you would expect a certain reaction such as the hands dropping down to protect the area being struck. The same can be said when aiming a punch to the head, so long as you are aiming at the target and are accurate when hitting it, you will cause your opponent to assume either a *reactionary* or *prone* position once struck.

Reactionary and prone positions can also be achieved with various foot and hand combinations such as a sweep and strike-down as in the technique **DANCE OF DARKNESS**. Alternatively, a very simple combination such as a basic front jab and right cross could be used to destabilize your opponent. The simpler the execution of your technique the better. Whatever the combination of basic moves you use, **ACCURACY** must always be used consistently when applying your technique. Knowledge of these positions and how your opponent is likely to react when hit, completes an important subdivision in your vocabulary of motion.

PRONE POSITION

Prone positions are extremely dangerous, they are vulnerable positions that you or your opponent may end up in once in a semi-conscious or unconscious state. If you are unfortunate enough to find yourself in this position, you will almost certainly have been hit extremely hard and may not be able to defend yourself effectively. Any impact that has the power and potential to knock you out must be taken seriously, it is not *tough* to carry on training if you have been knocked out by a shin kick to the side of the head. A byproduct of such a strike could be a concussion or a possible bleed to the brain. If you have been knocked out, even whilst training, an enforced period of rest should be adhered to. A concussion is your main concern after an injury like this, so watch out for signs of it, even if you have been hit in the head whilst training.

A concussion occurs when the head sustains a hard blow or strike, the resultant impact jars the brain inside the skull, interrupting the brain's normal activities. Symptoms of a concussion can range from being severe too mild. Depending on how serious the injury is, symptoms will usually develop within the first 24 hours after the incident has occurred. These can last from a day to several weeks following the injury and if you are in any doubt if you have suffered a concussion you should consult a qualified doctor to assess any symptoms you may have.

Although cuts and bruises may be visible on the face or head, it is impossible to see if a brain injury has in fact occurred, as there may be no physical or visible signs of a brain injury. If you are sparring make sure you always wear safety equipment. A head guard, groin protector and gum shield are all mandatory to train safely.

Signs and symptoms of a concussion may include:

- A headache or a feeling of pressure in the head
- Temporary loss of consciousness
- Blurred or double vision
- Confusion or feeling as if in a fog or fussiness
- Amnesia surrounding the traumatic event
- An inability to remember what happened
- Dizziness, lightheadedness are all indicators
- Ringing in the ears
- Nausea and vomiting
- Asking the same question over and over

IMPORTANT:

Remember if you are in any doubt with regards your ability to continue training, always take the precaution of consulting with a physician before you commence training again.

REACTIONARY POSITION

Reactionary positions are an inevitable part of combat. If you hit someone or they hit you, a reaction will take place. Whether it is a realignment into a more superior combat position or a placement into a more vulnerable position, it is simply a case of **"Cause and Effect."** It is a position that either person involved in combat can assume or be rendered into before, during, or after an offensive or defensive maneuver has been used. In laymen's terms, it simply means that if I kick you in the groin and use accuracy correctly and contact is made with the target, the person getting kicked will react accordingly. This might mean that they drop to the floor and assume a **PRONE POSITION** or they might turn and bend over into a **REACTIONARY POSITION**. A slightly more sophisticated way of describing it is that it is a relationship between actions or events that one or more are the result of the other or others. There are many advantages to practicing self-defense techniques, one of them is the development and attainment of knowledge of how your opponent will react to certain stimuli when using feints or strikes. Having knowledge of various positions that your opponent may end up in can be the difference in surviving a confrontation on the street or becoming a statistic of it.

Reactionary positions can be created by:

- Pushing your opponent away from you
- Grabbing them towards you
- Using sweeps to take them to the floor
- Setup maneuvers that destabilize them
- Strikes that cause a backward reaction
- Strikes that cause a forward reaction
- Locks chokes and holds that restrain your opponent

Bear in mind that the reactionary position of your opponent is based on your ability to be consistently accurate with both your application of strikes and blocks, however you can in most cases predict that your opponent will react in a certain way by striking certain targets in a  particular predetermined sequence or order. The application of your Kenpo skills is very similar to a pool or snooker player in the way they will automatically setup up the next move in their sequence of play. To a certain degree, they can predict how the game will play out due to the accuracy of their shots, and how they will line up the next move, knowing that accuracy is a basic fundamental that must always be applied to ensure victory, is fundamental in winning the game. A Kenpo practitioner uses the same strategy when setting up their next strike or block as this will render an opponent into a *reactionary* or *prone* position. This is the equivalent of setting up your next move in a game of pool.

ANALOGY - PINPOINT ACCURACY

Accuracy is not defined just by the target being struck or the block that is used to stop a strike. It is the precise application of **ANGLES,** and the ability to hit **VITAL TARGETS** at will, that defines accuracy. Throughout his teachings, Senior Grand Master Ed Parker would use various methods to convey a specific subject or point. He would frequently use the analogy of a boat and the ability to cause its demise and sinking, by an accurate well-placed shot to its hull.

"Do not practice to miss your target,
- be accurate and hit it hard"

The shot must be placed at or just below the waterline, how quickly the boat would sink would be dependent on the size of the hole that was created, and its placement in proximity to the waterline. Both of these elements would determine how long it would take to sink and the amount of damage that was created. Even if it was a small hole placed accurately just below the waterline, it would lead to the eventual sinking of the boat. This analogy is a great tool to pictorially describe the effect a well-placed strike would have on an opponent if accuracy was used and the **VITAL TARGET** that it was aimed at struck with the correct amount of power and force.

"Remember, you are only as good as your last training session"

CHAPTER 6

ANGLES

- The space between two lines or planes that intersect -

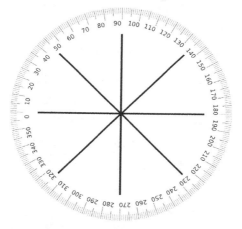

Angles are so important when delivering your offensive and defensive techniques, whether it is a punch, kick, or block. They are a degree of approach to targets that you or your opponent can use to strike from or too. They allow access to your opponent's **VITAL TARGETS** as well as giving you the ability to limit access to your own, they should also be viewed not only from your point of view but from that of your opponent's as well. They are an integral part of **ACCURACY** and it really doesn't matter if you are applying a lock, choke, or striking your opponent's vital targets, the angles that you chose when fighting can open up the availability of targets that you might not otherwise have access to. Angles are a measure of degree and are used in every aspect of your training. From the correct angle of your front foot in the application of a forward bow stance to the correct angle of your elbow that allows access to your opponent's targets. They are integral in protecting your own **CENTERLINE** from strikes whilst gaining access to your opponent's. For example, gaining access to your opponent's rib cage for a sidekick might only be achieved by using a back fist to the head first using a feinting technique, this, in turn, causes a reaction whereby they lift their front arm, this would then allow a new **ANGLE OF ENTRY** for your sidekick. The same principle can be applied if you were to strike with a reverse punch.

There are many subdivisions of angles that will enhance your knowledge of Kenpo and your ability to use it effectively in a street environment. Angles can be subdivided into certain categories that give the practitioner of Kenpo a greater understanding of how the application of them can enhance strikes, open up target areas, and generate more power.

They include the following:

- **ANGLE OF ALIGNMENT**
- **ANGLE OF CANCELLATION**
- **ANGLE OF CONTACT**
- **ANGLE OF DEFLECTION**
- **ANGLE OF DEVIATION**
- **ANGLE OF DELIVERY**
- **ANGLE OF ENTRY**
- **ANGLE OF DEPARTURE**
- **ANGLE OF DISTURBANCE**
- **ANGLE MATCHING**
- **ANGLE OF NO RETURN**
- **ANGLE OF RETURN**
- **ANGLE OF OBSCURITY**
- **COMPLEMENTARY ANGLE**
- **ANGLE OF INCIDENCE**
- **SURFACE CONCENTRATION**
- **CONTOURING PRINCIPLE**

Angles are defined as part of the motion chart which can be viewed in my first book Kenpo - How to Survive Life for further reference.

ANGLE OF ALIGNMENT

An angle of alignment refers to the adjustment of the path of your weapon in reference to your opponent's targets. This is essential to give it proper alignment and perspective. An example would be the pointing of your knee to its target before you execute your kick or the lining up of your shoulder and elbow behind your fist before you execute your strike.

ANGLE OF CANCELLATION

An angle of cancellation if used correctly will nullify your opponent's ability to strike or grab you. It puts them in a position that restricts their ability to use natural or man-made weapons to strike you. Ideally, their height, width, and depth zones would be canceled with your action. This could be force meeting force, or the use of an angle of deflection where the force used is riding or deflecting their action.

ANGLE OF CONTACT

Using the correct angle of contact can enhance the power of your strikes, an angle of contact can be any angle that achieves this action. It can also be dual in purpose, however, it is not always possible to maximize your strike by landing it with a perpendicular angle that will increase the power of your strike, specifically an angle of incidence.

ANGLE OF DEFLECTION

This entails using a block or parry to deflect an attacking weapon away from the target it is intending to strike. The idea that you should block an attacking weapon before it gets close to you is the foundation of this subdivision. Mr. Parker would use a saying to elaborate on this principle. **"To beat action, meet it."**

ANGLE OF DEVIATION

This is the use of angles to get out of the line of attack. It is used extensively throughout your training to give you the best angle of attack once you have moved off the line of your opponent's attacking weapon. An example of how this can be this applied is in the self - defense technique **Attacking Mace**.

ANGLE OF DELIVERY

An angle of delivery can be any angle that you deliver your weapon from, so long as it is used with **accuracy** and hits the target it is aimed at. It should be efficient in its motion (economy of motion) and is effective in neutralizing your opponent.

ANGLE OF ENTRY

If an angle of entry is used correctly, it will allow access to your opponent's targets from specific angles and paths which can be executed on a horizontal, vertical, and diagonal path of action. This is also true if the role is reversed and they are attacking you.

ANGLE OF DEPARTURE

Do not complicate your movement or your understanding of angles to the point they become ineffective and meaningless. The application of this angle is simply the use of foot and body maneuvers that will move you out of the way of an attacking weapon whether this is man-made or empty hands. For this angle to be effective, you must use the most desirable angle to move away from your opponent and escape from them. This can be accomplished through the use of body and foot maneuvers that are combined with stance changes that move you out of the effective striking range of your opponent. Bearing in mind that if your opponent is using a weapon your range will increase or decrease accordingly.

ANGLE OF DISTURBANCE

Backward Momentum

Elbow to throat

Buckle to rear of knee

An angle of disturbance is a very useful tool to have in your arsenal of weapons. It is primarily used to upset and disturb your opponent's balance thus making it difficult or impossible for them to launch an effective attack against you. It has many practical applications and can be applied in a multitude of ways. This can include a front hand grab to your opponent's wrist that pulls your opponent down on a diagonal plane. Leg sweeps that take out the base of your opponent, and strike-downs as in the above picture that uses stance changes combined with strikes to unbalance your opponent. Strike-downs being the preferred option instead of a passive take-down. Your opponent's body naturally has pivot and fulcrum points that you can use to your advantage. If you push in one direction whilst pulling in the other, an unbalancing of your opponent's body will take place. You can destabilize your opponent by placing your hip against their hip, as in the above picture, the rear of your opponent's leg is then buckled as you drive your leg back into a forward bow stance, this is carried out at the same time you execute a strike, pull, or grab at chest or head height. Remember if you strike high, you must destabilize the lower height zones of your opponent. Regardless of the method used, the desired result is to cancel out your opponent's ability to retaliate.

ANGLE MATCHING

This non-contact method of ***contouring*** uses the concept of complementary angles to enhance your strikes. This is extremely useful in delivering a weapon to its target using your opponent's own body as a guide to specific vital target areas. An example would be an inward horizontal elbow strike to the rib cage using your opponent's arm as the guide to the target area. You must never take for granted the ability to see your target properly. Your senses play an important role in how you deliver your technique and which targets you are able to strike. If you are attacked in a dimly lit environment, using angle matching to gain access to your opponent's vital targets may be your only chance of actually hitting them.

COMPLEMENTARY ANGLE

Having the ability to strike an opponent's vital targets with power is the end goal for any martial artist. Any angle that helps achieve this should be used to complement this action. A complementary angle is one that parallels an opponent's attacking weapon and helps guide your weapon to its target. It is a *non-contact* method of contouring and is used in conjunction with angle matching.

ANGLE OF NO RETURN

Learning how to use your body weight to complement your fighting ability is integral to everything you do as a martial artist. There are times however that it becomes illogical, impractical, and awkward to retrieve the momentum you have generated and place it back to its point of origin. This is especially true when using a step-through punch or kick, and generally refers to the angles the upper body and hips go through when blocking or striking.

ANGLE OF RETURN

As stated in the previous section, that it becomes illogical to return your hips and upper body to its original position once it has gone through an *angle of no return*. An angle of return, however, refers to the upper body and hips having the ability to return to its original point of origin and continue to fight from it. As you move forward your body momentum and weight stop at a non-committal point in your action. You then have the option to move to any angle that you desire.

ANGLE OF OBSCURITY

As far as angles go, this is probably one of the most used when fighting. It is the use of specific angles that obscure a weapon from being seen by your opponent. This can be achieved a number of ways, your body can be used to conceal the weapon and the path it may travel on, or your opponent's own body can be used to obscure the weapon as it travels to its target.

ANGLE OF INCIDENCE

If you want to increase the amount of power that you can hit a target with, try to use a perpendicular angle (right angle) when you land your strike. This is the point where your natural weapon makes the correct and proper angle of contact with your target. Two important factors occur when the correct angle of delivery is applied. The weapon maximizes its force by causing surface concentration and penetration to occur together. This can have a different effect on your opponent depending on which method of striking is employed.

This could be either **SNAPPING** or **THRUSTING**. Snapping involves the fast retraction of your weapon out and back to its original position, thrusting, however, requires that the weapon terminates past its point of contact and locks out. If for example, you use a punch to strike a target it can use both methods of *impact concentration.* As the fist hits its target, the knuckles will penetrate deep into the muscle tissue whilst the whole fist will add to the amount of surface damage that will occur. This can only take place if the weapon used is accurate, and hits its target at the correct angle. If it was to "skim" its target the desired result might not be achieved.

SURFACE CONCENTRATION

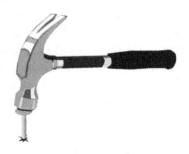

Combat and the angles that are used to access targets are not just about how hard you try to hit something, it is also concerned with the amount of force applied to the weapon being used and the target that is struck. The amount of stress that is inflicted on the surrounding area, and the damage that is caused because of it. A commonly used analogy to highlight this point is the use of a nail or a pin. The end of a nail or pin is extremely small, this means instead of it concentrating its energy across the surface being struck, and being dissipated across a wider area, it has a **"pinpoint"** effect that drives it deep internally. A hammer striking a nail will drive it deep below the surface, this principle, if used correctly, is much more penetrating, and will cause internal damage rather than external damage, so long as the weapon you are using is striking with a small surface area. An example being a finger poke to the eye or ridge hand strike to the groin or throat. The use of a knife or stabbing weapon would also have the same devastating effect on a soft target.

CONTOURING

Using the concept of contouring to access targets on your opponent's body, is a valid and important combat tool if used in conjunction with an overall understanding of angles, and how they can enhance your strikes or locks.

It involves using the outline of your body or that of your opponent to gain access to vital targets. Your weapons are delivered using **BODY CONTACT** methods such as fitting, gravitational checks, leveraging, pressing checks, and sliding checks. **NON BODY CONTACT** methods include angle matching, framing, complementary angles, symmetrical angles and silhouetting. One example of a *non-contact* method would be to use the contour of your opponent's leg to guide your kick to the person's groin. A *body contact* method of contouring could be the use of a back fist that fits the contour of your opponent's cheekbone. As you can see in the picture, the knuckles fit perfectly into the bone structure, just under the eye socket. The idea is that you literally fit the weapon to its target using the natural curvature of the body part that is being used and the target that is being struck. Using this method will enhance the effectiveness and power of the strike.

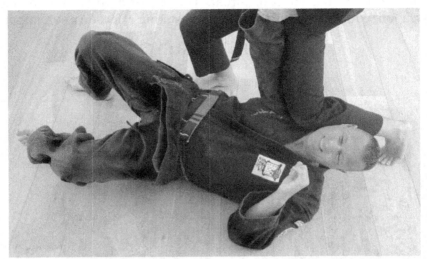

The offensive use of a close kneel, fitting the shin and knee across the neck

As you train in Kenpo, you will quickly learn that there are many techniques that show less obvious paths and lines of action that are sometimes missed by the naked eye. The fitting of weapons to targets, is just one example of how using the correct angle at the correct moment in a fight, can have many far-reaching residual effects. Although we should always practice with speed, fluidity, and timing, the addition of striking at the correct angle at the right time, will help gain valuable seconds in a real fight on the street.

The fitting of weapons to specific targets is not isolated to the upper body alone. The use of height zones to drop a knee strike onto a downed opponent's neck is also considered as contouring. As the knee fits into the curvature of the neck, it can be considered as a ***body contact*** method of contouring. The offensive use of stances and the ability to strike a downed opponent using knee strikes as well as close and wide kneel stances are an extremely useful component in your repertoire of motion.

CHAPTER 7

BODY ALIGNMENT

- The act of adjusting or aligning parts of a body in relation to each other -

It is an accepted part of any martial art system that you must have correct body alignment when delivering your strikes or blocks. Having incorrect alignment will lead to an unstable stance and a noticeable decrease in power. Always consider that a house is always built from the foundations upward, which is why you must spend time training not only strikes and blocks but the mechanism that will deploy them, which are your stances and the correct alignment of them. This simple basic, combined with the correct body alignment will allow you to produce stability in your stance whilst producing maximum power in your strikes. When you train, try to place an equal amount of emphasis on your training that develops your natural ability to *feel* that you have the correct alignment before, during and after you apply a technique.

Always consider the alignment of your opponent in relation to yourself

Standing with your feet too far apart, or to close together will all affect the effectiveness of a strike. Try not to stand in your fighting stance with your elbows kicked out to the sides, this action will expose your rib cage unnecessarily and leave you exposed to a strike. This slight misalignment can leave you open for a side-kick or punch that could do serious damage to your rib cage. One rule of fighting is to always keep your elbows down as fighting is effectively the sum total of all the concepts, theories, and principles that you have learned. These are then applied in the most efficient format that will increase your chances of winning a fight. Having the correct alignment from the ground up is essential for this to happen. As far as training is concerned, you should be concentrating on your stances and footwork first. The next areas to concentrate on are your hips and shoulders. Kenpo has a wide variety of stances that are used depending on the combat situation. Kenpo's base stance and the one you will always revert to is the **neutral bow stance**, or **fighting horse stance**.

Left neutral bow shown

This stance forms the foundation from which all other stances are derived from, your weight distribution is divided equally between both legs, fifty percent on the front leg and fifty percent on the rear leg. The knees are kept slightly bent with the heels pushed out for added stability. If the right side of your body is forward, the neutral bow is called a right neutral bow. If the left side is forward, it is called a left neutral bow. The hips and shoulders face a 45-degree angle one way, whilst your feet face the opposite direction also at a 45-degree angle. This effectively makes an imaginary multiplication sign on the floor that you visualize you are standing on. This is a very useful tool to obtain the correct alignment of your upper and lower body. Your spine should be in a natural neutral position without twisting it when in this stance. Your hands should be placed in a guard position in front of your body, the lead hand above the rear hand. From this position, you have maximum protection, whilst still being able to use your rear hand and leg to defend or attack with. Do bear in mind, that your stance must also be functional, and that you must be able to maintain your balance whilst using strikes whether they are empty hand techniques or handheld weapons. Remember you must be able to strike from this stance using **POWER** whilst still moving at **SPEED** and hitting your target.

You can always see the martial artist who has achieved good body alignment through their training. They move effortlessly from one move to the next whilst striking and blocking with power and accuracy.

"If it doesn't feel right, then it isn't right"

Visualize body alignment as the correct coordination of body parts that follow the correct angles of travel so they move together in the same direction, thus increasing the amount of power that is generated in a block or strike. Developing the correct alignment will not only ensure your stability from the correct anatomical alignment of your stances, shoulders, and arms, but it will increase the **SPEED** at which you deploy your movement.

Body alignment allows the application of other key principles to be applied in combat with efficiency and effectiveness. Placing your feet, hips, and shoulders, at the most optimal **ANGLE** allows this principle to be combined and applied with the most effect. This principle will also trigger the application of **BACK-UP MASS** (Chapter 8), this is the enhancement of your strikes by using your body weight to add power to your action. Having incorrect body alignment when moving, will most definitely affect how you can apply your technique. It is a priority principle that should always be applied and adhered too. Body alignment is not isolated to the martial arts alone. It is universally applied to everything we do in life. From swinging a hammer that drive's a nail into a piece of wood, to the skateboarder who must maintain balance along with the correct body alignment to perform stunts.

CHAPTER 8

BACKUP MASS

- A body of matter without definite shape -

Although I covered this subject in my first book Kenpo - How to Survive Life, it is a basic principle that should always be applied when striking and moving your body forward, backward or to the side. Striking or blocking with the mass of your body behind and backing up your weapon will add power to your strike, it is as simple as that. It is the whole *mass* of the body that generates power, not just the weapon or block that is being used to strike with. It is simply the whole of your body weight directly behind the action that is taking place. You don't just hit with your fist when you land a punch, you focus on using the whole weight of your body.

THE BUMPER AND THE TRUCK

One of Mr. Parker's favored analogies that he used extensively to emphasize this point, is the bumper and the truck. He would always ask this question when studying the momentum generated by a truck, "if a truck was to hit you, would it be the bumper or the truck that strikes you."

Most people would instantly assume that it is the bumper, of course, the bumper is connected to the truck, so that will hit you first, but the logical answer is that it is the whole truck that will hit you, not just the bumper. The bumper is only the means by which the energy that has been created is transferred along with its momentum that hits you. This is the same for a punch, kick, elbow, or knee strike. There are many examples that use this principle, a kick delivered with your hips and torso moving forward and directly behind the action will apply this principle effectively. The same thing applies when a punch is thrown with the weight of the body behind it.

You must also consider that your opponent will try to apply the same principles as you, even if they do not have the same terminology to explain what they are doing, they will still understand that by pivoting their hips and swinging their shoulders forward, they will generate enough power to render someone unconscious. There does not need to be any finesse about the application of this priority principle. It simply needs to be applied throughout your training so that the practitioner of Kenpo, understands that to generate power in any given situation, your body weight needs to be behind the action that is taking place.

CHAPTER 9

ECONOMY OF MOTION

- The efficient use of resources, the economy of effort -

Being frugal with your money and economizing on its expenditure is at the base of any good financial management plan. Getting more for your money than another person is good economics if applied with prudence and frugality. The same principles are also applied when fighting, if you flail your arms and legs around without being accurate and do not hit your intended target, then you have **WASTED MOTION**. If however, you were to use the shortest possible route and use the correct **ANGLE** to strike your opponent's targets, then you would have **ECONOMIZED** on your motion, you simply did not waste your energy or movement in doing something that was effectively a waste of time and effort. The martial arts are full of analogies and stories that emphasize this principle, it is not new, it is however sometimes forgotten about when teaching the vast amount of techniques and principles that Kenpo contains. Try to develop your fighting skills using this principle to reduce the amount of time it takes to execute a move and disable your opponent's ability to retaliate.

ANALOGY OF:
PRINT - SCRIPT - SHORTHAND

One particular analogy that is useful in explaining this subject is the use of Print, Script, and Shorthand writing skills. These three different forms of writing can be compared to motion in its three different states. Solid, liquid, and gaseous. There are many different ways a person can write our written language, with each person having a distinct writing style of their own.

PRINT
SHORTHAND
SCRIPT

Just as each person has a unique way of writing, their martial art skills are reflected in the same way. The basic principles of technique application remain the same for every practitioner of the arts, however, the way they are applied is as individual as a person's handwriting skills. Some people have a basic understanding of how to speak and articulate our written language, whilst others have a much greater understanding and meaning of the written words and can articulate them at a much higher level. Professional speakers are considered to be in this category. The foundation of your training will start as print writing, it will naturally progress into more fluid movements such as script writing eventually progressing into shorthand. Your goal as far as motion is concerned, is to shorten your moves into as few as possible by combining them together. You can execute a sweep with a strike, or apply a lock with a choke as you're going to the ground. This can also apply to restrict your opponent's movement by using a pre-emptive strike that is applied with a grab or block. This could be a kick to the groin, just as your opponent chambers for a kick, or just before your opponent's kicking leg has hit the ground as in the technique **Thrusting Salute**. Although your movements at a beginner level will resemble print writing, it will naturally progress towards more fluid script motion, the more you learn and ingrain movements into your subconscious mind the more fluid your movement will become. Ideally, the desired result from your training will consist of a combination of all three stages of writing, print, script, and shorthand.

PRINT

Print writing can be considered as the execution of your basics whilst being pronounced phonetically one move at a time. They are articulated as individual syllables that can be compared to individual moves within your vocabulary of motion. A simple block or punch executed as a single move can be used as an example.

SCRIPT

Scriptwriting, on the other hand, is more fluid and continuous; the letters are joined together in one continuous flowing motion. Many times script writing will retrace the same path or move onto the next letter without stopping. Motion uses this same principle when moving from one move to the next in a technique sequence. You may use the same paths and lines of motion and may even use the same ones many times over for the same technique, but they are executed with fluid and continuous motion.

Shorthand

Shorthand writing is condensed and contains many of the same attributes found in print and script writing whilst being direct and straight to the point with many meanings in one syllable, thus taking much less time to write. If we apply this same logic to training in Kenpo, you will see the relationship between shorthand writing and the principles that each technique contains. We want to cut down on the amount of time it takes to achieve an action when applying it to our training, eventually acquiring the knowledge to apply it in a self-defense situation on the street.

POINT OF ORIGIN

Another concept that has great value is to move your block or strike from its **POINT OF ORIGIN**. This can be accomplished by practicing to strike from where your weapon is located directly and moved directly to its target. To increase your speed, and your ability to beat your opponent's action, it is essential that you **do not** chamber a weapon back in the opposite direction before executing it. There is however always an exception to this rule, especially if your intention is to use the chambering of the weapon as a feint prior to your intended action. Unless your weapons are already moving at speed and are already in motion, you simply punch or kick from where the weapon is, its original point of origin. In doing so it will increase your speed and power as other principles come into play. Your goal is not to use motion that would otherwise expend your energy unnecessarily, but to use movement that cuts down on the amount of time and energy that it takes to defend yourself. This is the core principle of economy of motion. If for example, you use a punch to strike with, make sure you aim your weapon directly at its intended target, the same applies to a kick; make sure you get into the habit of pointing your knee at the target before you start to extend your leg. By developing strong core basics, with good habit's such as moving your weapon from where it is, rather than chambering it back in the opposite direction, you will decrease the amount of time it takes to execute a strike. Never forget that the other person will be trying to hit you back! This fact alone should always to be taken into consideration when fighting. Never underestimate your opponent and never give them the opportunity to initiate a surprise attack by using economy of motion against you.

"To beat action you need to meet action"

Remember to **RELAX** in-between strikes and do not waste time on throwing out a weapon that has no chance of reaching or hitting its target unless of course, it is a deceptive move that sets up a major move. Do not overreach to meet your opponent's punch or kick, by doing so you may unintentionally cause yourself to become unbalanced and expose your target areas unnecessarily. Committing yourself to an action that has no chance of succeeding is wasting time and energy, instead, you should be comfortable by meeting your opponent's attack by staying in balance and in focus.

Economizing on your motion is not isolated to strikes alone, it is implemented across all aspects of your training. From footwork to stance changes and kicks, all these elements benefit from movement that is direct and applicable to the situation that it is being used in. This principle will not only speed up the application of your upper body strikes, but it will also increase speed across all areas of your training. So make sure when you train, you include motion that is not only logical when applied to a self-defense technique, it is applied with correct *body alignment* and *focused power* as well.

CHAPTER 10

TIMING

- The regulation of occurrence, pace, or coordination to achieve the desired effect -

TIMING, A COMPARISON TO MUSIC

Music is not played at one constant note, it changes constantly, it is sometimes slow like a ballad, or extremely fast like dance music. This change in rhythm can be compared to the change in the timing of your strikes, at a basic level they are never delivered at a constant speed, they change as the situation changes depending on whether the threat is severe or not. Kenpo is never static, it is delivered at lightning speed with coordination between the upper and lower body combined to maximize power. It is the timing of this coordination and how it is applied that makes Kenpo an effective and direct martial art. It requires that you block or redirect an aggressive action then strike simultaneously or immediately afterward and continue to do so until the threat is neutralized. This requires you to use **DISTANCE** to your own advantage by entering or exiting the effective striking range of your opponent at will. This will include knowledge of your own height, width and depth zones and how changing them whilst in combat will influence any counter-attack initiated on your opponent. Developing the ability to strike any target at will must be done with the correct timing as you are constantly moving in and out of combat ranges using the timing of your footwork to achieve this action. To generate **POWER** in your strikes, it is essential to have the correct **BODY ALIGNMENT** combined with **COORDINATION** between your upper and lower body. However, this must also include the correct use of timing between your upper and lower body also.

MAXIMIZE YOUR EFFORTS

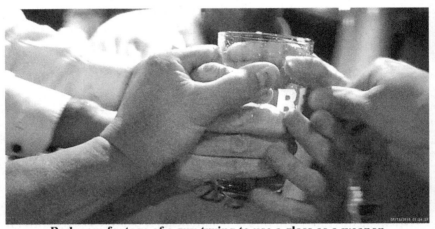

Bodycam footage of a guy trying to use a glass as a weapon

Never forget that the *timing* of your breathing whilst striking or moving must be synchronized and combined with the exact moment you settle your body weight. It is an important factor that should never be overlooked when training. If you are to maximize your efforts and actually hit your target, exhaling sharply whilst punching or kicking, will not only add power to your strikes, it will also add mental focus to your action. This will inevitably increase your overall mental awareness of your situation and the environment you are in. However, the effectiveness of your strike will be drastically reduced by using incorrect breathing patterns as you land your body weight with your punch. All elements of your training must be synchronized to work as one unit. Incorrect timing will dissipate your energy reducing the amount of power you would expect to generate when applying the principles of **BACK UP MASS** and

BODY MOMENTUM alone. It is not enough to land a strike with all your body weight behind it, then move to your next strike at an even quicker pace without considering the timing of not only your strikes but the retaliatory efforts of your opponent as well. If you move too soon you will **TELEGRAPH** your move, move too late and they may be faster than you and land their own strike first.

The initial start of a fight is the most critical, it is at this point that you should have already established if your opponent has the necessary skills to inflict serious harm to you or your family. My own personal experience working the door is that it doesn't matter if it's a huge guy or a small girl, the stature of a person is not irrelevant if they catch you on the blind side of your vision, or they smash a glass in your face when you are not looking. So make sure you pay attention to what is going on around you as you walk down the street or are out in a bar, don't take it for granted that nothing is going to happen. If a conflict does take place, this is when you should be moving at full speed using a flurry of strikes that hit your opponent's **VITAL TARGETS**. Your strikes should always be aimed at targets that will render the greatest effect in the shortest possible time. Once you have some sort of control over the situation, you can change the timing of where and how you apply your strikes, locks, chokes, and holds on your opponent. Make sure you practice on the heavy bag.

This is all done at a subconscious level, you do not even have time to think about what you are doing, you must just react to any technique that is thrown at you. This is where your knowledge of **RANGE** combined with the correct use of *timing* that is essential to your overall understanding of the principle and how it affects your response to any given situation.

CRITICAL TIMING

Cancels depth zone

Knee cancels the leg

As combat constantly changes, along with the speed and technique your opponent uses, the chances of you keeping the same speed or rhythm is remote, it will increase or decrease depending on the scenario and the type of attack you have encountered. You would not keep striking at the same speed as various factors will come into play such as stamina and physical ability, changing the rhythm of how you strike, along with where you strike, is intrinsically linked to the weapons you will also use. You could say that timing is the sophistication and punctuation of rhythm. If you were to use incorrect timing, you would not achieve maximum power which could reduce your chance of victory.

FLASHPOINTS

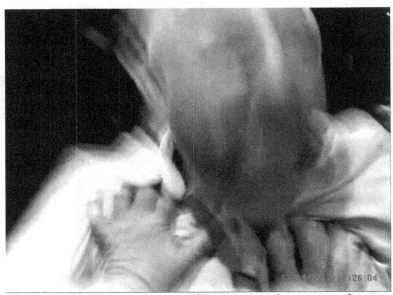

Actual footage from my bodycam pushing an aggressive guy away from me.

The above picture is a still taken from my bodycam at work. The persons face is blurred out to protect their identity, however, this incident warranted me removing them from the premises and pushing them away from me once outside as they came forward to assault me. The timing at this point is critical if you are to prevent getting head butted in the face, or punched in the head. Although this is a still picture this all happened in a fraction of a second. Timing is not just about how fast you move and how quick your reactions are. It is just as important to assess a situation and make the right decision in how you deal with it. Do you enter into a confrontation with someone over something trivial, or do you simply walk in the opposite direction? You need to be able to recognize potential *flash points* as well as the risks involved in dealing with them. It is your mental and physical timing that should work together to resolve these potential escalations from an emotive verbal confrontation to actual physical violence. The point at which you leave an area of conflict or intervene in a fight can be critical to the outcome of such an event.

Important practical considerations that you should always include as part of your timing skill set is to develop the following areas of your training:

---

1. **Assess the situation for severity.**

2. **Escape from the area or situation.**

3. **Evade your opponent's strikes.**

4. **Move out of the line of attack.**

5. **Bridge the gap between your opponent(s).**

QUARTER BEAT TIMING

This type of timing is used throughout your training in Kenpo, it is the application of strikes that use one quarter beat timing which is used to disrupt an already established rhythmic pattern. This can be used to disrupt the flow of your opponent's punching techniques and combinations by using *striking checks* to limit their ability to retaliate. This type of timing is especially useful in techniques such as **Parting Wings** and **Five Swords** where one move immediately triggers the next move. This can also be used where a check is inserted in the sequential flow of action that renders an opponent's limb temporarily immobile for a fraction of a second. Sometimes the speed at which you are moving disguises these subtle inserts and changes in timing, in many cases it is only the trained eye that can see these changes and react accordingly to counter them.

Having worked on the door for over 13 years, I have seen plenty of confrontations that should never have escalated to the point that physical intervention was needed. There is a point in any argument that you should consider walking in the opposite direction and removing yourself from the environment that you are presently in. The *timing* of this action can be a mitigating factor whether you end up in court or not. A simple miscalculation at this point could see you in a prison cell for grave and criminal assault simply because your ego would not let you walk away in the opposite direction. The streets of towns and cities are not the Octagon and they are not the Dojo. They have laws that apply to everyone that walk on them and if you are caught committing a crime you could be charged with any number of offenses. Agreeing to have a sanctioned fight does not carry the same type of risk.

"Kenpo teaches techniques, not for the sake of the technique, - but for the principles that are involved in the technique"

CHAPTER 11

TELEGRAPHING

- Communicate indirectly, by a change of expression -

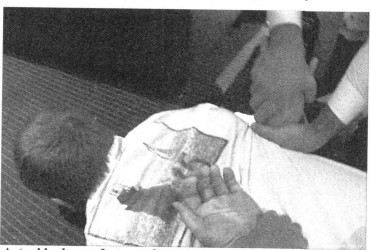

Actual bodycam footage of a restraint on an attempted glassing

Showing your opponent what you are about to do is not a good idea when you are about to strike them or defend yourself against them. It is often body language, along with verbal rhetoric, that will more often than not alert the opponent of your intended action. I was at work the other night and fight broke out just in front of the nightclub. The funny thing about it was not that the two guys were fighting, but one of them drew his arm so far back to throw a punch, that he might as well have sent the other guy an email telling him it was coming! The extent to which he telegraphed his move was staggering! His only saving grace was that he did it next to two police officers who quickly broke up the fight. It was certainly an education in how showing your hand too early in a fight could cause your unintended defeat, or at the very least limit your ability to counter your opponent. As the above description describes a real street scenario that actually happened, telegraphing your move is normally done with body language, you may move your foot too soon before you kick, or drop your front hand before you throw a right cross, or in this case chamber it back past your right shoulder. This type of telegraphing will work against you by physically showing your opponent what you are about to do, or intend to do. In doing so it will help them prepare an effective defense against you.

"If you don't show how will they know?"

Just like a card game, showing your hand to early in a fight whether it's in the ring or on the street can work for your overall defense strategy or against it, facial expressions that give away your intended move can be used as a deceptive strategy that can be used to disguise your intended counter move or offensive move. There are two ways to consider the use of telegraphing and incorporating it into your repertoire of movement.

1. The first is **defensive,** this entails limiting the use of any body or facial expression that might alert your opponent to your intended action.

2. The second is **offensive,** this is the effective use of deceptive telegraphing as a strategy to trick your opponent into exposing their **VITAL TARGET** areas thus enabling access to them for an effective strike.

In all of these scenarios, it would certainly alert your opponent to your intended action. It could also be an unintended facial expression that alerts your opponent to the fact that you are about to initiate an attack. All of these actions will give your opponent a chance to counter you before you have a chance to land your strike and vice versa. However, the use of telegraphing can also work for you by deceiving your opponent into thinking you are going to initiate a certain offensive or defensive move, only to change your mind at the last moment. This is the effective use of telegraphing using **FEINTS** and **DECEPTIVE MOVES** to confuse and baffle your opponent to what you actually intend to do.

The following methods of telegraphing should be practiced to develop your skill set:

- **DECEPTIVE FEINTS**
- **DECEPTIVE ACTION**
- **DECEPTIVE GESTURES**
- **DECEPTIVE RHYTHM**
- **DEAD MOTION PRINCIPLE**
- **DECEPTIVE FEINTS**
- **DECEPTIVE TIMING**
- **DELAYED MOVEMENT**

DECEPTIVE TELEGRAPHING

Feints are maneuvers designed with a specific aim, they are used extensively throughout your training to trick your opponent into opening up targets that they would otherwise vigorously protect. A great way to practice using deceptive moves is to add it as an integral part of your sparring program.

DECEPTIVE FEINTS

The use of deceptive feints is used to condition your opponent into reacting to a subconscious preprogramming of their mind. This ensures a planned reaction from them with the stimulus supplied by you. This could be repeatedly throwing a high back fist to get them to lift their front arm to expose their ribs for a kick.

DECEPTIVE ACTION

Deceptive action can be described as the use of feinting movements along with misleading and illusive gestures that confuse your opponent. For example, this could be the use of a double front jab that makes your opponent lift their front arm to defend themselves which opens up their rib cage for a strike.

DECEPTIVE GESTURES

Many times Kenpo will use terminology that is similar or identical to describe the same thing. Deceptive gestures are the type of moves that are included in deceptive action and feints.

DECEPTIVE RHYTHM

Deceptive rhythm is another term that is used for deceptive timing.

DEAD MOTION PRINCIPLE

This is an extremely useful form of deception, it involves the use of deceptive maneuvers that give the illusion that your weapons are motionless and inactive. The illusion that certain weapons could not reach your opponent or are at a standstill and of no threat to them is extremely useful in launching a surprise attack. It is used to ambush your opponent with offensive techniques from a **ZONE OF OBSCURITY**. When the action does happen it originates from an unexpected angle or zone which your opponent does not expect.

DECEPTIVE TIMING

Once again this can be used to great effect and is timing which causes your opponent to react to any given technique prematurely to the action you actually intended to use.

DELAYED MOVEMENT

This is timing that is used within your sequential flow of action that uses a pause to confuse your opponent. It is timing that is used to alter rhythmic patterns that motion contains. Quarter beat timing as described in chapter 10 explains this in more detail.

CHAPTER 12

COORDINATION

- The skillful and effective interaction of movements -

The key ingredient in developing coordination is repetition.

Having the correct coordination between your footwork and upper body movements is an essential component of your training. The effective use of it will aid your overall use of **TIMING** which in turn will allow you to function with more dexterity and continuity of movement. The key to developing intuitive responsive coordination is **REPETITION**. Even if you lack coordination at the beginning of your training, the more time and effort you put in the better your performance will become. You will not improve any aspect of your training by sitting at the side of the class and watching other people workout. You have to make the effort and get on the mat yourself, remember repetition is the mother of all skill.

COORDINATION - COGNITIVE STIMULATION

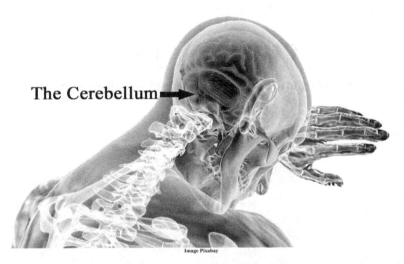

The Cerebellum

Image Pixabay

Brain function is an important aspect of your training that should not be overlooked. Motricity (motor function) along with the basic movement of the limbs, requires different areas of the brain to function correctly. The main part of the brain responsible for coordination is the cerebellum. The cerebellum is located at the back of the brain, just below the cerebrum. It is a very important part of the brain as it controls your balance, movement, and coordination.

For the majority of people, body movements are smooth, seamless and coordinated. However, even if you lack basic coordination this can be developed and learned through drills and practice. Nevertheless, in a very small percentage of the population, a condition that can cause a dramatic impairment or loss of coordination is referred to in medical terms as Ataxia. Having the ability to strike an opponent whilst moving at speed is not something that comes naturally to a lot of people. In many cases, students lack the coordination needed to perform the most basic of skills required to defend themselves. The great thing about training in the martial arts is that you can learn it relatively easily. Repetition is the mother of all skill, so long as you are willing to commit the time to develop the skills required to defend yourself then you should have no problem in developing coordination in your movements.

Coordination is often referred to in two parts:

1. The first part is the synchronization of all body parts so they function together as one smooth effective unit.

2. The second part is brain function combined with Motricity skills. This could come from the practice of self-defense techniques, forms or sparring.

Coordination is not confined to your body alone. Your opponent has the same functions, they may even have greater coordination than you that will make defending yourself against them much more difficult. They will try to use everything they have learned to defeat you in a fight. Whether it is on the street or in competition, disturbing the rhythmic patterns of your opponent along with how they execute their techniques is at the basis of any good self-defense system. The coordination of these functions need to be disturbed and stopped, this includes the weapon an opponent may use to strike you with, the direction it originates from, along with the target areas it is aimed at. As all of these considerations will have an impact on your conditioned response. The **SPEED** at which this information is processed at is then transferred to your limbs whereby an ingrained conditioned response is initiated. It is also useful to coordinate your moves with the **DIRECTION** an attack is coming from and the correct use of **TIMING** when executing your response. All of which will affect the eventual outcome of a fight.

COORDINATION SET 1

The great thing about coordination is that it can be learned, repetition is the only way to develop this aspect of your training which requires that you simply get on the mat and train. To help develop this aspect of a practitioners training, an individual set of movements was developed to improve the mechanism with which a strike or block could be delivered. This involved the blending of stances, blocks, and strikes that allowed the practitioner to flow from one move to the next with a clean clear upper and lower body coordinated process. Coordination Set 1 contains moves that singular in motion but may have a dual purpose. This includes the simultaneous delivery of strikes whether it is a block, punch, or kick. Although every aspect of your training will develop coordination in your movements, Coordination Set 1 was introduced into the American Kenpo system to give an appendix of motion for an intermediate student. The reasoning behind this was to purely focus on one key principle for the student to develop.

VIDEO

Coordination is not confined to upper and lower body movements alone, the use of hand combinations is also an integral part of your training and should not be overlooked. Not only does the integration and development of this part of your training improve your overall delivery process, it also improves many other key principles at the same time. Balance will automatically improve as your movements become more fluid and synchronized.

I have compiled a video of how to practice Coordination Set 1 in order for you have a working knowledge of how practicing this set can help your overall development in Kenpo. Instructions on how to access further videos on Kenpo can be found at the back of this book.

"Fighting spirit is often the dominating factor in a street fight, such instincts are born into an individual not learned"

CHAPTER 13

FOCUS

- The concentration of attention or energy on something -

Kenpo utilizes black dot focus

Focus can mean many different things to different people. In its physical form, it is the whole body working as a compact defined unit at the moment of impact. It is the culmination of all principles that generate power, this includes the synchronization of your mind, breath, and physical strength. Focus is not achieved in isolation, it must also include the method of execution when striking or blocking, along with the integration of all 21 key principles. This includes timing, penetration, coordination, marriage of gravity, and backup mass. In fact, it is the culmination of combining together all elements at the exact moment of impact that defines focus. Applying the correct *mental* as well as *physical* focus on your training whilst having an end goal to what you wish to achieve, is essential to achieve maximum results from your efforts.

Unlike backup mass that uses the weight of the limb directly behind the weapon being used, focus is the delivery of the whole body as a weapon. This includes knowledge of target areas combined with your actual physical strength, it is not just the application of a single physical move.

"Do not focus on one thing,
          - to the detriment of everything else"

MENTAL FOCUS

Image Pixabay

Mental focus is sometimes referred to as concentration, it is the cognitive ability of an individual to direct mental effort on the most relevant information in the environment they are in. The ability to focus is like a mental muscle, the more we work it out the stronger it becomes. Meditation at the beginning and end of a class helps develop this important aspect of your training. By clearing our mind of all outside thoughts, we enable ourselves to focus on the present moment and what is actually unfolding in front of us. If you are involved in any type of confrontation you must have the ability to act and function with a clear mind.

The more focused we are, the more successful we can be at whatever we do, this includes developing your ability to concentrate when learning the physical application of Kenpo. Conversely, the more distracted we are by outside influences the less well we do. It is the development of mental focus and the ability to stay concentrated on what you're doing, and not be distracted that is at the foundation of the most basic skills in anyone's mental toolbox.

The key to living a productive lifestyle lies within you building focus on what you wish to achieve, then simply doing it. Whether this is learning a new form or developing better timing in your techniques. Mastering your mental focus is your long-term goal in Kenpo and in the long run, it will create a more disciplined balanced you.

The majority of us tend to become a victim of our minds ability to wander onto other subjects when we should be concentrating on what's actually in front of us. This is a side effect resulting from doing too many things at the same time, in many cases this is a result of modern living where we are all juggling our time on multiple things, which ends up with getting nothing done. It is so important to concentrate on what's happening in the present moment, the ability to multi-task can only be achieved by focusing your mind.

TRAINING TIP 1: Focus on one thing

Multi-tasking causes the brain to load several bits of information at once. When the brain has to refocus, it drains the brain of energy leading to fatigue and the inability to focus. By focusing on one goal, you can conserve energy and become more productive. You should, however, try to develop the ability to multi-task as it will increase your ability to free flow within a technique sequence.

TRAINING TIP 2: Develop a positive attitude

Developing a **POSITIVE MENTAL ATTITUDE** can assist in the progress of building focus. Reinforcing your goals with positive affirmations will not only keep you calm and motivated, but you will remain focused on what you are doing and what you wish to achieve for longer. This is not isolated to your training but to the whole of your life and the way you wish to live it.

TRAINING TIP 3: Meditate to calm yourself

Meditation is the most powerful tool someone could use to build focus in their lives. Many people will fluff this aspect of training into something it is not, by simply making it mystical and unattainable. Developing the correct breathing technique whilst focusing your mind and clearing it of negative thoughts and distractions, is the key element to this aspect of your training. The use of meditation helps clear negative thoughts from your mind along with outside distractions. People will often bring negativity into your life, do not let other people sway you from your own goals because of their own shortcomings. By improving your mental focus and meditating at the beginning and end of every lesson, you are instilling calming and positive thoughts into your life.

This can be achieved by training yourself to simply watch people. Whether you are training in the Dojo or developing your skill level by watching people on the street, try to develop your senses so that you can see a situation unfolding before it has actually happened. Do not just focus on what is happening in front of you, use peripheral vision to focus on what is happening within a 180-degree radius of your body. When confronted with a violent or emotional situation, your brain will load the context of what you're doing into active memory, if you end up not concentrating on what you are doing and constantly switching your focus, you're actively forcing your brain to spend time it doesn't have in a stress situation to reload the same information repeatedly. The downside to this constant switching can be mental and physical fatigue. However, by spending enough time on developing your mental focus, you can avoid the waste of such energy, whilst developing a more balanced focused mindset.

BLACK DOT FOCUS

This is a valid concept used throughout your training that visualizes focus as a black dot on a white background. This represents **total awareness**, it does not focus on one point or target on your opponent to the detriment of your own self-protection. Instead, it promotes awareness of your **ENVIRONMENT** along with who is in it. This also includes potential weapons that could be used against you. It instills in the practitioner that they should not become **TARGET FIXATED** when using offensive or defensive techniques. Its primary aim as a teaching aid is to enforce the application of maximizing your power whilst striking a specific target, whilst gaining maximum protection at the same time. If you train with the attitude that you should *not* have to pay attention to anything else other than what is happening at the exact moment you execute your technique, you will most definitely leave yourself open for a counter attack.

The use of black dot focus may be better described through an analogy. It has all to do with paying attention and intention. When you train and focus on striking a specific target you can do so but you must also be aware of any other activity that may be going on around you. The use of peripheral vision is an integral part of this concept. Being alert and making sure someone does not blindside you with a strike from an **OBSCURE ZONE**, is critical for this concept to work. Simply focus on the target you wish to strike but also be aware that your opponent or a bystander may hit back! If you are able to strike your intended target or block your opponent's action whilst being able to see the counter punch coming, then you are using black dot focus.

WHITE DOT FOCUS

"Do not use tunnel vision in combat"

This concept of focus uses a white dot pictured on a black background. It represents **unawareness,** its main concern is striking a target with maximum power. This can be to the detriment and disregard for your own self-protection. Kenpo does not advocate the use of this type of focus in combat. There is value in using this concept as a tool for teaching students to be aware of their surroundings and to remind yourself of the same thing when you train. It is also a way of contrasting a broad vision concept such as black dot focus, versus a tunnel vision concept such as white dot focus. There is nothing mystical in using either form of focus to explain how a student should be practicing to strike a specific target, however, it is important to differentiate the use of either one when in combat.

Ok, if we recap for a moment, remember in Kenpo we visualize a black dot on a white background, thus representing total awareness. Our concern is not only in generating as much power as physically possible when we strike but in protecting ourselves as well. White dot focus, on the other hand, visualizes a white dot on a black background representing unawareness.

"Principles need to be altered,
   - to fit the anatomical makeup of an individual"

CHAPTER 14

POWER

- Force aided by concentrated focus -

Mr. Parker wrote power as the "magnification of force aided by concentrated focus." In layman's terms, it really means that physical strength plays an important role in how much power you generate when striking or blocking. Upon the impact of any particular weapon, your whole body needs to be in focus with it. Speed is also important and plays a significant role in producing power from a punch or kick, which is why Speed should always accompany the application of your physical strength. Power is not generated on its own, it requires a combination of many factors. It is also relevant and proportionate to the physical strength of a person executing a move and requires the channeling of physical force to a specific target. Our natural instinct is to always hit as hard as we can, the problem with doing this is that if you commit to full power in every strike you will almost certainly become fatigued very quickly in a street fight. There is also the possibility that you might over rotate and miss your target and expose your own target areas, the result of which could be disastrous in a real fight. It is much more important to know when to use full power and be able to control the use of it at the exact moment you need it.

Some important considerations when generating power:

- Never tense prematurely when striking, it will retard power
- Always use speed as an integral component of power
- Use maximum power with discretion
- Power can also cause damage to yourself through injury
- Speed contributes to increasing power
- Do not sacrifice correct body alignment to increase speed
- Do not expose target areas unnecessarily
- Apply principles consistently

If for example, you were to use full power in every strike when practicing in the Dojo you would soon run out of training partners that wish to train with you. Kenpo teaches its students to *control* the power of a strike not to *pull* the weapon before it makes contact. In doing so, it enables the safe practice of techniques that would otherwise cause serious injury to its practitioners.

Strikes aimed at **VITAL TARGETS** such as the throat, eyes, and groin, need very little power to inflict serious damage to your opponent. Which is why it is illegal to strike these targets in almost all competitions, the risk of permanent damage is simply too great. If you wish to develop and gauge how much power you actually generate, you need to hit the heavy punch bag. This is where you will be able to land strikes with as much power as you like, the only real risk of injury is to yourself. You must also be aware that the harder you hit due to an increase in **SPEED**, the more power you are likely to generate so long as you add penetration to the strike or block. Making sure you have the correct anatomical alignment through your bone structure is essential to prevent injury to your joints. Just because you can generate power, does not mean that you cannot be defeated in a fight, it simply means you have more of a chance of defeating your opponent if you make contact. The human body is an amazing piece of engineering, it can withstand unbelievable amounts of damage and then repair itself. There are many people that train who are extremely conditioned to absorb punishment to their bodies. If you come up against someone who is resilient to increased levels of pain you may need to strike with full power to **VITAL TARGETS** to beat them.

CHAPTER 15

TORQUE

- A twisting force - to turn in place -

Torque is defined as a twist or turning force on an object or body. It is calculated by multiplying force and distance. It is a vector quantity, meaning it has both a direction and a magnitude. Torque by definition is the application of force to an object on an axis. This could mean your car's transmission making the wheels turn, or your own arm turning a spanner that loosens a nut, unscrewing the top off of a bottle or turning the steering wheel on a car.

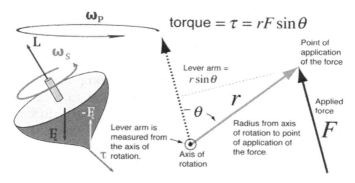

$$\text{torque} = \tau = rF \sin\theta$$

DEFINING MUSCLE TORQUE

Muscle torque follows the same basic rules, but it's slightly complicated by the body's own physiology. Force comes from a group of muscles, which produce movements by pulling on tendons, these in turn pull on bones. Almost all movements require several muscles working together in groups, most skeletal muscles are arranged in opposing pairs at joints. Muscles then move the body part in question by contracting and then relaxing. It is also worth noting that a muscle can only exert a pull and not a push. The axis point within this equation is the joint that's controlled by the muscles. In addition, another important factor in this calculation is the length of the limb or muscle group involved in applying the force, if, for example, you execute a back fist to your opponents face, the Triceps muscle's on the back of your upper arm would be used to extend the arm to its target, whilst the Bicep muscle's on the upper front of your arm would be used to pull the arm back. All of these factors come into play when calculating muscle torque.

This translates over into Kenpo by its very nature in that it is necessary to use the rotational energy of your body, arm, or fist to maximize **POWER**. Torque is an integral component in the production of power when striking or blocking. It is the rotation of your hips when kicking or punching as well as the rotation of your arm and fist when using a punch to strike with. It is defined as a twisting force that adds power to your strikes and blocks, although it is always desirable to use torque when striking, you can still produce a considerable amount of power even if you do not use it.

However, torque does play an important role in your development as a martial artist, and the amount of power that you can generate. Mr. Parker described torque as the *"preliminary stage of focus that adds to power"* and in reality, this simply means that if you add rotational energy to your movements it will increase your ability to generate more power with less effort. This is mainly due to the correct alignment of your bone structure along with the muscle groups involved. You must also consider the fact that you are bringing into play different body parts at slightly different time intervals.

For example, if we look at how torque is generated when striking with a reverse punch, you will see that the rear foot rotates slightly before the hips, which in turn rotate with the shoulders. The fist is rotating at the same time as you rotate the hips and shoulders, but the timing of it is slightly ahead of your elbow. The result is that the application of torque can be at different time intervals, and at different stages in the execution of the punch.

This is just one example of how the rotation of a specific body part can produce more power by simply unifying it with another principle. As you can see by this example, torque actually takes place at several different locations on the body and uses a relay system to apply it. It is also necessary to combine torque with other principles to enhance its action. It is not initiated on its own but part of a unification of principles that increase **POWER** in general. It is also important that it is applied with **SPEED** as this will invariably alter the effectiveness and depth of your strike. All of which may enhance the outcome of a fight.

EXAMPLES OF THE APPLICATION OF TORQUE:

Hand-sword (inward)
Hand-sword (outward)
Ball Kick
Roundhouse kick
Sidekick
Reverse punch
Front punch
Back Fist
Overhead downward elbow

Do not lose sight of the fact that you can also apply torque using the lower half of your body as well. The application of knee strikes and stance changes combined with the dropping of your body weight as you rotate your hips, will all produce extra power. When training try to develop this principle so that it is applied instinctively, this will increase the speed of a technique which in turn will increase your power.

OTHER EXAMPLES OF ROTATION:

Rotational force - a revolving action that aids to power
Rotational chamber - the rotating of the body or limb to a more advantageous position that will produce more power
Twist - to rotate or turn in place
Rotate - to revolve around a common axis point
Rolling - using 180 and 360 degree
Rolling Check - the use of body contact using rolling to control your opponent

ROTATIONAL FORCE

Rotational force is described as a revolving action that aids to your overall use of power with the result that torque is a byproduct of it.

ROTATIONAL CHAMBER

A rotational chamber is the rotating of the body or limb to a more advantageous position that will produce more power when either a block or strike is executed. This could be part of a technique sequence such as Five Swords, where the flow of action enables a continuous combination of strikes, blocks, and checks with torque being applied from one move to next.

ROTATE

To rotate involves revolving around a common or central axis point around which anything rotates or revolves: It is the center or middle point that is used as a point, pivot, axis, etc.

TWIST

The definition of twisting is to rotate or turn in place. This is the application of torsional stress that can be used when locking and restricting the movement in a joint that will cause the breaking, dislocation, spraining or distortion of it. Locks are applied when you have entered **CONTACT MANIPULATION** range and wish to limit the ability of your opponent in striking you. This is a close range application of torque.

ROLLING

Rolling is applied in two distinct methods, vertical and horizontal. It is defined as moving by turning repeatedly on an axis using 180 and 360 degree's movement this is another valid method to increase and apply **BODY MOMENTUM**.

ROLLING CHECK

The application of a rolling check is useful in the prevention of an intentional or unintentional strike from your opponent. It is the active use of your limbs or body that stays in contact with your opponent's body. Its purpose is to stop his intended or otherwise action and literally entails rolling from one point on your opponent to another without leaving contact with them. It is the use of body contact using rolling to control your opponent and minimize their ability to retaliate.

CHAPTER 16

BODY MOMENTUM

- An impelling force or strength, mass in motion -

It is very easy to define the technical side of fighting when having to describe **GRAVITATIONAL MARRIAGE** or **BACKUP MASS**, body momentum can be best described as momentum that is used to increase **POWER**. It is the uniting of your mind, breath, and physical strength whilst moving forwards or backward using shuffles and foot maneuvers that are executed using horizontal motion. It can be defined by its use of transitional foot maneuvers and stance changes to generate power. It is the mass of the entire body, not just a portion of it such as a limb.

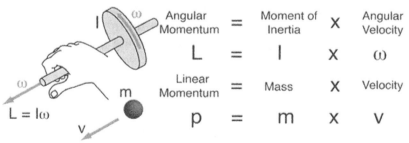

Angular Momentum	=	Moment of Inertia	X	Angular Velocity
L	=	I	X	ω
Linear Momentum	=	Mass	X	Velocity
p	=	m	x	v

$L = I\omega$

The **X** implies simple multiplication here.

The mass of the body when executing a strike is greatly enhanced if used in conjunction with other *priority principles*, such as **GRAVITATIONAL MARRIAGE**. The use of it if used in conjunction with **SPEED** will greatly increase the impact of mass, this will also depend on the weapon you are striking or blocking with. Physics defines the symbol for the quantity momentum as the lower case p. Therefore the above equation can be rewritten as $p = m$ x (x is considered as simple multiplication) v where m is the mass and v is the velocity. The equation illustrates that momentum is directly proportional to an object's mass and directly proportional to the object's velocity. A mass unit is multiplied by a velocity unit to provide a momentum unit. This is consistent with the equation for momentum. Consider a truck and a bicycle moving down the street at the same speed. The greater mass of the truck gives it a considerably greater momentum.

$$p = m \text{ x } v$$

Yet if the truck were at rest, then the momentum of the smaller bicycle would be the greatest. The momentum of an object that is at rest is zero and has no momentum. Objects at rest do not have momentum they do not have any **mass in motion**. Both variables, mass, and velocity, are important in comparing the momentum of two objects. When you move forward backward or to the side you create body momentum. You simply need to be moving to create momentum which in turn will create power in your strikes.

Momentum can best be defined as a mass in motion.

$$p = m \text{ x } v$$

Momentum = mass x velocity

The standard metric unit of momentum is the kg m/s. While the kg m/s is the standard metric unit of momentum, there are a variety of other units that are acceptable. It becomes obvious that an object has a large amount of momentum if both its mass and its velocity are large. Both of these variables are of equal importance in determining the momentum of an object at impact. Especially when a strike or block is applied in Kenpo.

CHAPTER 17

GRAVITATIONAL MARRIAGE

- Vertical Momentum -

This is one of the most easily recognized principles used throughout the Kenpo system. It is literally the marrying of your breathing, the application of your physical strength, and the focus of your mind uniting together to maximize your power and energy. Its basic concept is that it uses gravity to enhance the effectiveness and power of your strikes. All of these elements are combined together and used simultaneously whilst dropping your body weight vertically. This is the use of body momentum on a vertical plane that utilizes the dimension of height to generate power. Depending on the weapon being used, it can strike to a number of targets depending on whether your opponent is standing vertically in a fighting stance, on their way to the ground, or is already laying in a vulnerable or prone position on the floor.

GRAVITATIONAL CHECK(S)

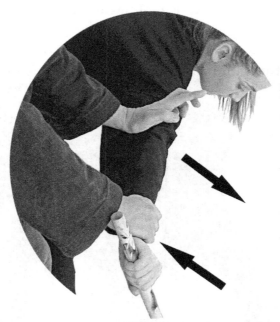

Gravitational check at the elbow in Obstructing the Storm

Gravitational checks fall under the category of **CONTOURING**. They use parts of your body to leverage or pin your opponent's limbs and prevent them from obtaining height which would otherwise give them the ability to gain an advantage, as well as leverage over you. An example of the use of gravity to aid your downward momentum can be found in the self-defense technique ***Obstructing the Storm***. It can also be found in the self-defense technique ***Grasp of Death*** as it is used to pin and strike the back of your opponent's calf and knee joint. The dropping of your body weight at the correct moment is essential to prevent your opponent from gaining leverage for the headlock and choke. The **TIMING** of your moves are critical if you are to apply this principle effectively. In the following example, a close kneel stance is used as a strike and check to the shoulder. This can also be applied to the arm to pin it to the body, or the head and neck in more extreme circumstances.

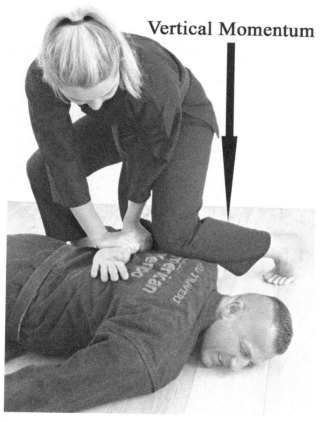

Vertical Momentum

Remember that **GRAVITATIONAL MARRIAGE** can also be referred to as **MARRIAGE OF GRAVITY**. In many cases, the terminology is interchangeable and means the same thing, the basic concept is that when you strike and drop your body weight, gravity will help increase power in your strike. Therefore, you literally have a marriage of all elements that contribute to generating power. Using this principle teaches you to generate power on a vertical plane utilizing your body weight as the mass behind the motion. The effect of which will be to increase power whilst blocking, striking or pinning your opponent to the floor. The addition of diagonal motion will also add additional depth to your action which, in turn, will trigger the principle of **BACKUP MASS**.

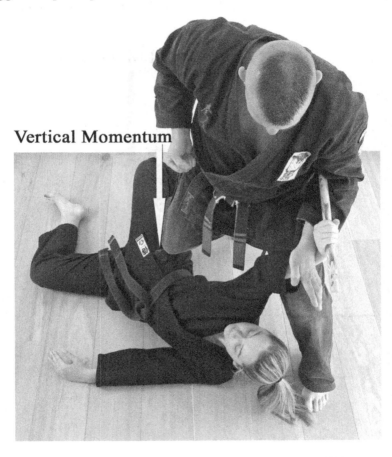

Vertical Momentum

There are many examples that can be used to illustrate this principle. It is instinctively used throughout Kenpo self-defense techniques and can be considered one of the main *priority principles*. I have used this extensively over the years working the door, it enables you to pin and restrain an opponent whilst using your whole body weight to do so. This is an essential principle to learn.

CHAPTER 18

PENETRATION

– The depth to which something penetrates, especially the depth reached by a projectile that hits a target –

Penetration generally refers to the depth a weapon has when hitting its target. It stands to reason that if you have only practiced punching and kicking in the air, shadow boxing, or practicing forms, you will not have developed your muscle structure to withstand the force of impact that hitting a solid target will give. Hitting something solid is very different to practicing techniques in the air. Which is why it is so important to hit focus mitts and the heavy bag as part of your training. Neglecting this part of your training could have serious consequences later on in your development as a fighter.

It would be like practicing to shoot a gun, aiming it at a target, squeezing the trigger, only to shoot blanks all the time. At some point in your training, you must have the feeling of shooting live rounds if you are to feel the full recoil of the weapon being used. This is the only way to develop accuracy in your shots. Not only is it essential to develop your stances when shooting, but it is also essential to learn how to breathe and exhale at the correct moment. These are the same principles that are applied in Kenpo when executing a strike if the depth of penetration is to be achieved.

Punching the heavy bag is the only real way to feel how hard you can hit something and feel how much penetration the strike has. Settling your body weight whilst breathing out, and bringing into play all the principles you have learned, is the only way to feel how hard you can hit, and the amount of power you will generate in doing so. Penetration can best be described as the impact point of your weapon in relation to the surface of the target being struck. It is the depth of focus used whilst using power to hit a target. It should be considered as a ***priority principle*** in that it should be used in all circumstances regardless of whether it is a block or strike used in a defensive or offensive situation. It is also worth noting that it is also relevant to the distance you are fighting from and increases the amount of power used in the delivery of your weapon if it is accompanied by **SPEED** and **FOCUS**. This is the impact point that terminates an inch or two beyond the surface of the target that is being struck. As mentioned previously, we do not strike to a target in Kenpo, we strike through it. How far your strike penetrates into your opponent will depend on many factors, the target that is being hit and whether it is a soft tissue target or a hard bone structure such as the skull or jaw.

PENETRATION POINT

    Incorporate into your training routine, ways in which to visualize this point, so that you do not prematurely tense before the moment of impact. Doing so will only retard your ability to produce power from your strikes. However, if followed correctly, this principle will not only increase the amount of damage inflicted on your opponent, but it will increase your power in proportion to the technique being used as well. As stated in Chapter 6, penetration may take place an inch or two below the surface being hit using a pinpoint effect or dissipated over a wider area depending on the weapon being used.

"Train with specific goals in mind,
    - Logic and Practicality should head your list"

CHAPTER 19

TRANSITION

- The stage between moves - moves within moves -

    Footwork along with stance changes allow you to move from one strategic position to another with fluidity and flow. These transitional moves bridge the gap between parts of a technique sequence to another and are an essential component of motion, as they allow the practitioner to move with **SPEED** and **POWER**. They are transitional bridges of motion that enable you to move from an **OUT OF RANGE** position, to **WITHIN RANGE** of your opponent's vital target areas. Once these first two ranges have been bridged, you can then enter into **CONTACT PENETRATION** and **CONTACT MANIPULATION** range. This could simply be a transitional foot maneuver such as a step-drag that immediately drops into a close kneel stance or a stance change that increases or decreases distance.

TRANSFORMATIVE MOVE(S)

Transformative moves are moves that have the ability to deceptively change the element of a move that your opponent sees to another move that will confuse or fool them. This is done using various methods which includes **BODY CONDITIONING, FEINTS**, and **DECEPTIVE MANEUVERS**. The purpose of which is to confuse and disorientate your opponent so they react to a conditioned response in a certain way. The use of transformative moves is essential in creating height width and depth deception to open up your opponent's target areas.

A simple example would be to throw a high back fist that your opponent reacts to by raising their front arm to block it, you then slide up with a side kick to the rib cage. The final move could also be a reverse punch, hook kick, ball kick or any number of moves that add to the **SEQUENTIAL FLOW** of your action.

TRANSITIONAL MOVES

Think of transitional moves as the links in a chain, when all the links are forged correctly they form a strong continuous process and can be likened to script handwriting (Chapter 9). However, they are only part of a bigger bond of connection between moves, however, they are still an important and integral part of the transitional process. Nevertheless, they are moves that are used to fill **DEAD SPACE** or areas of motion that would otherwise create gaps in your movement patterns and technique sequences.

CHAPTER 20

DISTANCE

- The amount of space between two things points or lines -

Distance is a numerical measurement of how far apart an object is in relation to each other. It is the amount of space between two things points or lines. In self-defense terms, this is how far away your opponent is from you and what effective action you can take in defending yourself or initiating an offensive move against them. Knowing the critical distance someone is away from you can make the difference in getting hit or not. As you see from the above footage from my bodycam, this guy was getting to close and entered into my personal space. At this point, I pushed him away to prevent him from staying within **CONTACT PENETRATION** range. He could have quite easily punched me from this range. This situation happened in a fraction of a second, you do not have time to think about what you are going to do you must react immediately to any potential threat. Hence I pushed him out of my personal space. Distance, if used correctly, can enable you to gain access to your opponent's targets, it can also work for you or against you. It can be your friend or your enemy depending on the circumstances it is used in. Your attention to detail especially the environment that you are in is fundamental in creating distance away from your opponent when a threatening situation occurs or decreasing it when you initiate a strike or block.

Critical distance is the distance that you or opponent can initiate an attack from, it is controlled by using foot and body maneuvers that are not only functional but effective in their application. They enable both yourself and your opponent to function in the third part of **RANGE** known as **CONTACT PENETRATION**. Remember this is the range that places you or your opponent within striking distance of each other. It is a critical range that must not be taken for granted.

CHAPTER 21

COVER

- A form of transition -

Notice how your foot realigns over the line of attack, this is the correct method

COVER STEP

This foot maneuver is used extensively throughout your training in Kenpo. Start by shifting your front leg to the opposite side of your body, this will aid you in facing the opposite direction. It is used to protect and conceal the groin area whilst covering and stepping in the opposite direction you are facing. It is normally executed from a neutral bow stance and helps the practitioner to change direction whilst using a stance change to protect the groin area. It is neutral in so far as you do not increase or decrease your distance in relation to your opponent. Once the footwork has been executed, it will place you in a position of readiness in case of another attack from the same or multiple opponents. Covering is a transitional maneuver that allows you to change direction allowing you to regain a defensive position ready for combat. It can be considered as the repositioning of your body into a defensive mode that creates distance away from your opponent whilst protecting you at the same time. It does have some residual benefits from the momentum that is created from this maneuver. As you turn you will create **TORQUE** from the rotation of your body, this can then be synchronized with a strike or block as you turn and move away from an attacker. If you have more than one opponent it is vital that you place yourself in a protective defensive position as much as possible. This foot maneuver is designed to move you away from a confrontation and into a safe zone away from your opponent. You are not turning into an attack as you are stepping away using your front foot, always make sure you look before you move as you may be moving into a punch or kick. When practicing self-defense techniques or forms, you will find that you are continually transitioning from one move to the next using a combination of foot and body maneuvers. This enables you to realign your stances and change direction at will. However, if you were to use your rear foot to step with, you would leave your groin open as you step to realign align your toe and heel over the line of attack. This should only be used in exceptional circumstances.

INCORRECT

CHAPTER 22

A TRUE STORY OF VIOLENCE

This is a true story about a friend of mine. I am sure that many of you that read this will be able to relate to the situation that he found himself in. First off, let me say that he had every opportunity to walk away from this confrontation and leave the area he was in which would have prevented this situation ever happening in the first place. However, that didn't happen.

One night in 2017 a friend of mine went out clubbing, he was out with his girlfriend and another male friend. They went to a local nightclub, had a few drinks, whilst at the bar another male, who was quite drunk, started a confrontation with them. As the situation escalated, the doormen went over and ejected the confrontational male out of the club. He then proceeded to wait for my friends outside. As they exited the club, the drunk male once again started a confrontation with him. This became even more serious when the male allegedly threatened them with a knife. As the situation had escalated even further my friend decide to try and de-escalate the situation and invited him around the corner to talk the situation through and find what the problem was.

As he turned round to face the male, the drunk man lunged at my friend with a punch. As he was trained in Thai Boxing he retaliated with a flurry of blows that sent the drunk male to the ground. He then continued the fight by pulling the male's coat over his head and proceeded to punch him repeatedly whilst he was on the ground. You can see the same techniques every day of the week on Sky TV or any M.M.A fight. The difference is they are in the ring not on the street. As the aggressive male had now been neutralized and no longer posed a risk to my friend or his girlfriend, he left the scene of the incident and returned home. As he walked away a police van came round the corner and found the semi-conscious male on the floor. Obviously, the correct thing should have been to stop and inform the police what had just happened, and in an ideal world, that's what would have happened. But we do not live in utopia, instead, my friend went on holiday, he came back after three weeks straight into the arms of waiting police officers at the airport.

CONSEQUENCES

So how did this happen? Well unbeknown to my friend there was a single HD - CCTV camera mounted on the wall above him that he did not see on the night in question. The footage of the alleged assault was then given in evidence to the police, one of the police officers recognized him and his arrest was ordered in his absence.

This is where it really starts to become interesting. Yes, he should have walked away and in no way am I condoning what he did. But it is somewhat peculiar in how the judicial system will allow two people to beat each other unconscious in a ring, just because a referee is present, and they arrest someone for doing exactly the same thing on the street defending themselves against a potentially life-threatening situation.

My friend genuinely felt that the threat to stab him was real and that the other male had a knife and was prepared to use it, so he protected himself fearing he was going to get stabbed.

So here is the dilemma in this situation, we are taught as martial artists that we should defend ourselves and protect our loved ones. He did just that, but what the martial codes of conduct do not take into account are the laws of the land that exists today. In the time of the Samurai, the law of the land was fight or die trying.

It is ironic that when you genuinely defend yourself you can end up in court with a charge of assault against you and the person who instigated the assault walks free. Ironically, two weeks after he threatened my friend, the same male was arrested for allegedly fighting again. The case against my friend was very clear, it was caught on high definition video and there was no doubt that he had a fight with the guy. What it does not show are the moments before when the male allegedly threatened to stab my friend or the provocation that started the whole incident in the first place.

My friend was charged with grave and criminal assault, the case went to court where he pleaded guilty to the charge. It cost over

£120,000 to defend himself, an astronomical amount of money when all he needed to do was walk away in the opposite direction. He was sentenced to community service and avoided a prison sentence as he pleaded guilty to the offense.

LIFE CHANGING

The story does not finish there, his whole life has been changed due to someone threatening him, as a martial artist he did what he has trained years to do, protect himself and his loved ones. One stupid act of violence has changed his life forever. Training in the Dojo and competing in a sanctioned tournament is not the same as fighting on the street. There are laws that are upheld by police officers who may themselves have ulterior motives to have you arrested and prosecuted. Not all police officers are fair, honest individuals, which is simply a fact of life.

My hope is that if you have read this you might learn something from my friend's mistake. He should have walked away in the opposite direction, he knows that now, and can repent at leisure whilst reflecting on the amount of money the court case has cost him along with the stress it has created in his life. Was it worth it?

He himself admits that he could have walked away in the opposite direction. Which really comes down to one thing, training in the Dojo is *not* the same as a sanctioned fight, and a sanctioned fight is *not* the same as fighting on the street. They are all very different environments with different rules affecting the outcome of a fight. If at all possible always walk away from a confrontation, fighting on the streets should always be the last resort.

It is a fine line between fighting to defend yourself against some person or persons attacking you in your own home, on the street, or in the subway, to actually getting prosecuted yourself. The violent criminal is not bound by the same rules that the ordinary citizen has to abide by. They do not care about you and they certainly do not care about the law.

Unless you are the victim of an unprovoked attack, always consider choosing to walk away from a confrontation unless you are prepared to justify your actions in a court of law. It takes a far better person to walk away from a confrontation than to walk towards it.

"There are no rules in a street fight,
- just a court of law at the end of it"

CHAPTER 23

CONCLUSION

This is the third and final book in this series on Kenpo. I hope that I have given some facts as well as historical data on the system of Kenpo and how it should be applied logically and realistically in today's environment. It is important throughout your training, that you never lose sight of the reasons why you are learning a martial art such as Kenpo and the intrinsic value it brings to your life. The 21 principles contained in this book should be used as the foundation of how to apply your technique in Kenpo, and more importantly how to generate power whilst doing so. The application of these principles throughout your training will greatly enhance your skill set and the execution of your own physical technique.

The fact that Kenpo is based on proven scientific principles that follow clearly defined structured paths, is at the very core of its historical success as a martial art and combat system. This enables the student learning the system access to *priority principles* that accelerate the learning curve with simple application and clarity. Through the practice of self-defense techniques, forms and freestyle fighting this leads to an enhanced stage of learning that teaches the student to react to any given situation intuitively.

The order in which strikes or blocks are applied is down to a combination of factors that will in the most part be down to the skill level of the practitioner executing them. However, the simple application of clearly defined principles within the structure of self-defense techniques is a prerequisite in having the actual ability to fight on the street. Principles acquired through training should be applied to a self-defense situation spontaneously and without thinking, this mindset can only be achieved through dedicated practice that develops the necessary skills to fight with. Every instructor will apply the same principles that are found in Kenpo, they may, however, prioritize them in a different order or rearrange the sequence they are executed in so that they tailor them to their own physical makeup. They may also add *signature moves* of their own into a technique sequence, thus ensuring the personalization of the technique and the instructor teaching it. Many times, you will see students of a particular instructor move, and you will immediately recognize who their instructor is merely by the way principles are applied and the technique executed.

Throughout this series on Kenpo, I have tried to consistently emphasize the need to be realistic about your training, try not to get caught up in the flash application of a technique without ever having an understanding of how applying it in a real conflict environment is *not* the same as drilling the technique in the Dojo. The execution of flash fancy techniques that look good in this controlled environment might get you killed on the street.

A seasoned street fighter who has been fighting in this environment all their life knows that they must hit their opponent as hard as they can whilst inflicting as much damage as possible. This must be done within the first few seconds of a fight to prevent the other person from hitting them back and gaining an advantage over them. They are never looking for flash nonproductive moves, just pure violence that renders their opponent incapable of retaliation in the shortest possible time. Every day we are bombarded with news articles that contain horrendous acts of violence, as you live your life try to develop spatial awareness to recognize flashpoints that could potentially contain this threat.

Kenpo is not just a self-defense system based on prearranged technique sequences, it is a system based on proven scientific principles that work. There are no rules in a street fight with the variables too great to guarantee a successful outcome unless the application of *key priority principles* is applied.

Circumventing a physical confrontation should be a priority when out on the streets. Fighting in this environment can have devastating consequences for the average person, not only physically if injured in a fight, but financially as well.

Train safe and do not become a victim of violent crime.

Roy Travert

ACKNOWLEDGMENTS AND REFERENCES

The author would be happy to receive any comments, including criticisms and suggestions, noteworthy comments may be included in any future revisions or updates to books of this series. To register a comment please visit our website www.jerseykenpo.com and navigate to the contact page.

To purchase further copies of this book, please visit Amazon.com or Amazon.co.uk. It can also be purchased through any of Amazon's European outlets. If you enjoyed reading this book please write a review of it on Amazon and tell your friends.

To view training videos mentioned throughout this book, please visit https://www.jerseykenpo.com and register as a member. You will then be sent a username and password to access the member's area of the site.

The author would also like to thank the following contributors for the use of their graphics throughout this book.

Freepik.com - Spine pictures
Freepik.com - Soldier Designed by kjpargeter / Freepik
Vecteezy.com - People pictures by Insanity
logoopenstock.com - Freevector finger print
Pixaby.com - Public domain free graphics
Clker.com - public domain vector clip-arts

REFERENCES

Ed Parker – Infinite Insights into Kenpo Series
Ed Parker – Encyclopedia of Kenpo
Ed Parker – Zen of Kenpo

Other titles by Roy Travert.

Kenpo - How to Survive Life
Kenpo - Eye of the Storm

Made in the USA
Las Vegas, NV
07 December 2023

82266898R00089